Museum of Fine Arts, Boston

The Deutsche Bibliothek holds
a record for this publication in the
Deutsche Nationalbibliografie;
detailed bibliographical data can
be found under http://dnb.ddb.de

Library of Congress Control
Number is available

Prestel Verlag, A Member
of Verlagsgruppe Random
House GmbH

Prestel Verlag
Neumarkter Str. 28
81673 Munich
Germany
Tel +49 (0)89 4136-0
Fax +49 (0)89 4136-2335
www.prestel.de

Prestel Publishing
900 Broadway, Suite 603
New York NY 10003
USA
Tel +1 (212) 995-2720
Fax +1 (212) 995-2733

Prestel Publishing Ltd
4 Bloomsbury Place
London
WC1A 2QA
UK
Tel +44 (020) 7323-5004
Fax +44 (020) 7636-8004
www.prestel.com

ISBN 978-3-7913-4693-9

Museum of Fine Arts, Boston Foster + Partners

Norman Foster
Edward R Bosley

PRESTEL
MUNICH · LONDON · NEW YORK

The crystal spine . . .
and the extended landscape . . .

Left: Norman Foster's sketch, articulating the concept of the 'Crystal Spine' and the idea of bringing the landscape of the Back Bay Fens into the museum.

Overleaf: The Art of the Americas Wing seen from the south-east corner of the MFA campus. In the foreground is Joel Shapiro's bronze, *Untitled*, 1997.

Introduction Norman Foster

The Museum of Fine Arts, Boston, or the MFA as it is known popularly, is one the world's finest museums, with a collection that encompasses 450,000 works, from ancient objects to contemporary art and sculpture. It is also one of America's most popular cultural destinations, drawing a million visitors a year.

As a physical entity, the MFA occupies a complex that has grown and evolved over many years since the first building on Huntington Avenue was completed by the Beaux-Arts architect Guy Lowell in 1909. In that sense, like the British Museum in London, or the Reichstag in Berlin, it can be thought of as a city in microcosm. Generally, the cities from which we derive most pleasure are not architecturally uniform, but they have a strong visual identity. However, while the MFA when we first came to it was stylistically diverse, the overall effect was incoherent.

Lowell's vision for the museum anticipated a complete circuit through the galleries – an intuitive route that relied on strong axes and clear vistas. Unfortunately, the building was never completed as he intended and subsequent interventions eroded the legibility of his original planning. The challenge, therefore, was to develop a masterplan that would allow the museum to expand while gaining a strong sense of being an identifiable whole.

We began by researching the building's history and analysing the impact of additions made by Hugh Stubbins and IM Pei, in 1970 and 1981 respectively. We also looked at the vital relationship between the museum and the city and examined how the building might be made more permeable and accessible, particularly in its relationship with the landscape of the Back Bay Fens – one of the links in Boston's Emerald Necklace designed by Frederick Law Olmsted, architect of New York's Central Park.

Lowell's plan offered us several clues. First was his north-south axis, with its sequence of grand reception spaces and dual entrances – one facing the city, the other opening on to the Fens. Curiously, this main route, which is so powerful architecturally, had been capped off. The Fenway Entrance, to the north, had been closed to visitors in the 1980s, which meant that nobody approached the building from the Fens. The loss of the Fenway Entrance and the opening of IM Pei's West Wing in the same period had the effect of drawing circulation westward, so much so that the majority of visitors entered via the West Wing. That shift had unintended consequences: the building's sheer size meant that the eastern end of the museum was atrophying, since most people never made it that far. It was clear that the composition needed to be rebalanced.

A further factor, which we identified with the museum, was the lack of a large, flexible space – a 'hub' – that could form a venue for major installations, host gala events or be hired out for large parties to generate revenue – a crucial consideration for a privately funded institution such as this.

Our starting point was to restore the north-south circulation axis by reopening the Fenway Entrance, making it fully accessible, and re-emphasising the Huntington Avenue Entrance as the museum's 'front door'. At the heart of this axis, beneath Lowell's magnificent rotunda, is a new information centre, from where visitors can begin their tour of the galleries.

Lowell's secondary east-west axis, which forms the centre-line of the museum and runs through two large courtyards, offered a further clue. These courtyards were originally open and had the potential to become a valuable amenity. However, given Boston's climate, with its harsh winters and hot summers, they were underused. We proposed sheltering the courtyards beneath glass canopies to create significant new public spaces, forming a 'crystal spine' at the heart of the building. We also suggested raising the courtyard floor level to align with the museum's piano nobile, thus establishing a new principal level which would allow visitors to move freely between the covered courtyards and the galleries – much as one does between the Great Court and the galleries in the British Museum.

In collaboration with the director, Malcolm Rogers, and his curators we analysed the MFA's collection and identified five principal focuses: the Americas; Asia, Oceania and Africa; Europe; the Ancient World; and Contemporary Art. From that analysis we developed the idea of five identifiable 'wings' within the museum, each related to a curatorial department and accessed directly from the main north-south and east-west axes. That was a significant step because the MFA is such a large institution: articulating it as smaller elements makes it far more intelligible.

The east-west centre-line became the guiding organisational device for the museum's long-term expansion. We arranged all the new buildings symmetrically on this axis, with the Art of the Americas Wing to the east and then a progression from public to semi-public to more private functions – conservation, study areas, and so on – to the west, culminating in a new home for the School of the Museum of Fine Arts.

Our strategy was to create the entire masterplan, so that it could be unfolded in future and then to focus on the first phase, completed in 2010, which involved the reworking of the museum from the east as far as the north-south axis. We were also able to reinforce the concept of five collections under one roof by consolidating the fifth collection – Contemporary Art – in the museum's West Wing.

The crystal spine encompasses the eastern courtyard, which creates spaces for visitor orientation and a café. Planted on two sides, the courtyard can be thought of as an enclosed garden, highly transparent and filled with daylight, which creates a social focus and gives the museum its long-desired flexible event space. From the courtyard, visitors access two new gallery elements: a temporary exhibitions gallery on the lower level and the Art of the Americas Wing. One of the museum's concerns was how to accommodate queues of visitors to its temporary exhibitions. The decision to locate the temporary exhibitions gallery beneath the courtyard was a natural step. It means that people queuing for admission can wait in comfort and relax, or have a coffee, whatever the weather.

Arranged over four floors – three above ground and one below – the Art of the Americas Wing contains fifty-three new galleries and has enabled some 5,000 works from the American collection to be placed on permanent display. Here, working closely with the curators, we looked at the way the collection would be arranged floor by floor, gallery by gallery. Long vistas, intuitive circulation routes and the sequential narrative of the collection – things that the original building communicated to us through investigation – led us to the final proposals. We designed each of the new galleries down to the smallest details of furnishings and the installation of the exhibitions; and the spaces are configured to allow the works of art to be displayed with an emphasis on clarity and light.

Three of the five 'wings' are signalled from the courtyard. We wanted to rely on as little signage as possible to indicate the different areas and instead to make navigation intuitive. Adjacent to the courtyard, a major piece of art announces each area of the collection so that one is always drawn by the objects. For example, a pharaoh in white marble stands at the entrance to the Art of the Ancient World. Similarly, within the new Art of the Americas galleries the visitor turns and sees a vista that directs the eye to a significant work of art.

An important consideration was to introduce transparency, both in the sense of opening up views for those in the museum and giving a hint from outside of the activity within. Approaching the Art of the Americas Wing from the park or the street one sees people moving between galleries and glimpses sculpture on each of the floors, reinforcing the notion of the art giving clues and drawing people in. For the visitor these glazed routes offer places to pause, with long views across parkland or downtown Boston.

The linear sculpture gardens we introduced between the courtyard enclosure and the existing facades serve a dual purpose. Firstly, we wanted to draw greenery into the space to evoke a sense of continuity with the landscape of the Fens. Secondly, Boston lies in a seismic zone. The historic buildings are not seismic compliant, which meant that either we had to upgrade the entire museum or build an independent structure that was seismically rated. The garden zones allow old and new structures to move independently of one another in the event of an earthquake; and the historic buildings will be seismically upgraded over time.

Museums for art, by their nature, require highly serviced spaces and the MFA's galleries are climate-controlled throughout the year. Nonetheless, we were able to implement a number of energy reducing measures. These include sun-shading devices to minimise the need for cooling; the maximisation of thermal inertia; the use of high-efficiency control systems; and relying on daylight and natural ventilation wherever possible. Behind the scenes, we put in place the infrastructure the museum needs for its long-term expansion, including a goods distribution network and a secure path for the movement of works of art. In place of a multitude of local plant rooms, there is a new state-of-the-art energy centre, which has reduced consumption significantly.

Our masterplan was potentially controversial in that it proposed removing some of the MFA's most recent additions, but the trustees understood that it was an essential step if the museum was to grow coherently. The public consultation process took several years, but once the proposal was in place, it was impressive to see how so many people bought into it, and at so many levels: trustees, benefactors, curators and museum staff, but also neighbourhood groups and the city and state authorities. The city went to extraordinary lengths to improve the surrounding roads and upgrade the landscaping of the Fens.

One of the things that struck me most, visiting the MFA after the Art of the Americas Wing had opened, was witnessing the transformation of the Fens. The fact that visitors are now encouraged to enter the museum from the Fenway means that the number of people using and enjoying the park has increased hugely. Together, through a civic and cultural partnership, the museum and the urban environment in this part of Boston have been transformed.

Cutaway drawing of the Art of the Americas Wing and Shapiro Family Courtyard with the North Pavilion in the foreground and South Pavilion shown complete. The extension reinforces the east-west axis through the original Beaux-Arts building.

Re-imagining the MFA Edward R Bosley

More than any other city, Boston symbolises the revolutionary spirit of the United States. The familiar dramas of the Boston Tea Party and Paul Revere's midnight ride – to alert colonial militia of approaching British forces before the Battles of Lexington and Concord – vividly characterise America's struggle for identity and independence. Modern Boston's thirst for intellectual, political and artistic innovation challenges even today the staid traditions of the Brahmin élite. From the radical essayists Ralph Waldo Emerson and Henry David Thoreau in the nineteenth century, to the Modernist émigrés Walter Gropius and Marcel Breuer at Harvard in the twentieth, the city and its environs have persistently explored the nexus of tradition and change. Now, the Museum of Fine Arts (MFA) – the pre-eminent icon among Boston's beloved cultural institutions – stands as a wholly transformed civic symbol of the old meeting the new.

The 'New MFA' marks Boston's most sweeping embrace of change in decades, integrating leading-edge design with the cherished legacy of the museum's historic buildings. It joins a family of transformational projects within the Foster oeuvre that complement heritage landmarks – a design discipline that has become one of the studio's particular strengths. The practice's development of principles in this field is perhaps demonstrated most dramatically by an early project, the Carré d'Art, Nîmes (1984-1993), which stands opposite the remarkably intact Maison Carrée – a jewel-like Roman temple dating from circa 16BC. The Carré d'Art not only embodied an architectural dialogue between ancient and modern but also provided a catalyst for the revitalisation of Nîmes, transforming a hitherto unloved square into a locus of vibrant civic activity.

Subsequent projects, such as the Reichstag in Berlin (1992-1999) and the Great Court at the British Museum (1994-2000), similarly challenged Foster to reinvigorate or 're-imagine' significant cultural symbols through design solutions that demonstrated sensitivity for heritage conservation and the environment. In much the same way, the once and future identity of the MFA, Boston, has been realised at a critical time in the institution's history as it re-asserts its historic role as the undisputed cultural focus of the city and as one of the great art museums of the world.

Architecturally, the MFA ranks among Foster's most comprehensive civic projects – a monumental, eleven-year expansion and renovation that has created dynamic synergies between classically-inspired heritage structures and a range of new galleries and public spaces. The public portal to the new exhibition

Right: The original Museum of Fine Arts building was a Gothic Revival structure, completed in 1876 and located on Boston's Copley Square.

Left: A view of the museum from Frederick Law Olmsted's Back Bay Fens, circa 1930. The James P Kelleher Rose Garden in the foreground was a later addition to Olmsted's original landscape for the Fens.

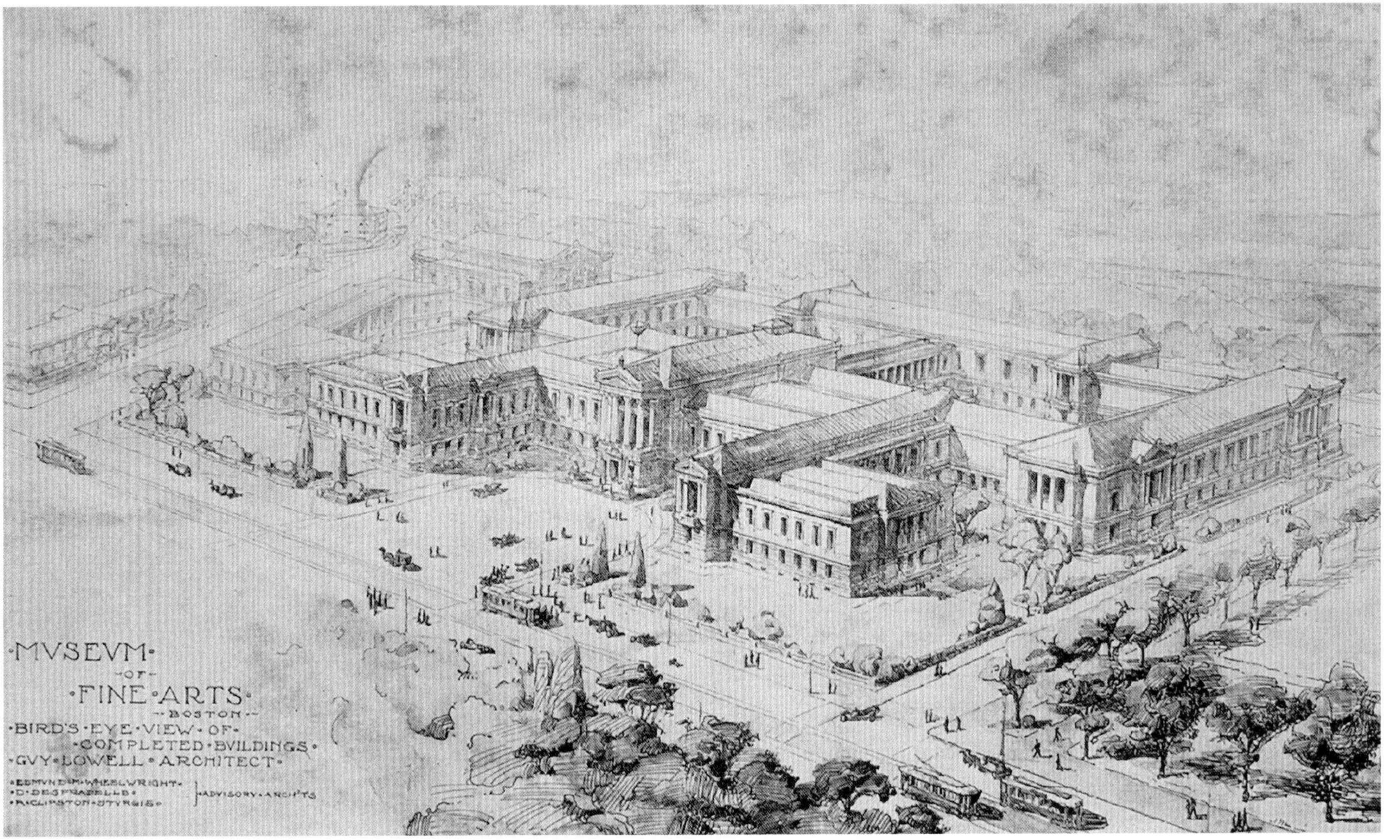

Above: Guy Lowell's original 1907 scheme for the Museum of Fine Arts. A Beaux-Arts composition, the building was intended to be constructed in phases. The site, close to the Back Bay Fens, was located in an emerging area populated with cultural institutions.

Above: An aerial view of the museum, looking north towards the Back Bay Fens. The photograph dates from the construction of the Decorative Arts Wing, completed in 1928.

Right: Completed in 1909, the Huntington Avenue building formed the first section of Guy Lowell's museum.

spaces in the Art of the Americas Wing is the soaring volume of the Shapiro Family Courtyard, which inspires social interaction while orienting visitors towards the MFA's collections. Curatorially, the Art of the Americas galleries challenge museum precedent; through the reinterpretation and integrated display of three millennia of art from North, Central and South America – a feat no institution has ever attempted before – the MFA's collections offer the visitor a compelling narrative of art along the length and breadth of the American continents.

For the Foster team – led by Spencer de Grey and Michael Jones – the starting point in creating the MFA's dynamic new spaces was a thorough study of the museum's history and the Beaux-Arts masterplan for the campus conceived at the turn of the last century by the Boston architect Guy Lowell. It is worth recapping that history here.

Before opening at its present location in 1909, the Museum of Fine Arts occupied a block-long, Gothic Revival structure on the south side of Boston's Copley Square – then called Art Square. Designed by John Hubbard Sturgis and Charles Brigham, the museum's fiery terracotta and red-brick edifice opened to the public on 4 July 1876 in celebration of the centenary of the United States. HH Richardson's massive Trinity Church stood on the square to the east, and by 1892 McKim, Mead and White's Boston Public Library had risen to the west. The elegance of Beaux-Arts structures captured America's imagination with the resounding success of the World's Columbian Exposition in Chicago in 1893. Indeed, the public's love of the Classical would formally shape the nation's civic image of itself throughout the early twentieth century under the rubric of the 'City Beautiful' movement.

However, by the 1890s the growth of the MFA's collections demanded more exhibition space than could be accommodated at Copley Square. Additional land there being unavailable, the museum's trustees secured a new site more than a mile to the west on Huntington Avenue. The museum's new home would be adjacent to the Back Bay Fens, a particularly sylvan portion of Frederick Law Olmsted's Emerald Necklace, the pastoral progression of urban parks which the eminent landscape designer conceived as garden-like links in a chain around the peninsular neck of Boston. By 1906 the trustees had commissioned Guy Lowell (1870-1927) to develop a masterplan to accommodate the institution's long-term needs on this new site.

Trained at the Massachusetts Institute of Technology and the École Nationale Supérieure des Beaux-Arts in Paris, Lowell was eminently qualified

Below: Guy Lowell's Beaux-Arts plan for the museum established strong north-south and east-west axes, with a clear processional circuit through galleries.

Bottom: The evolution of the museum. The Decorative Arts Wing of 1928 was the last building designed by Lowell. IM Pei's West Wing of 1981 deviated from Lowell's plan; in contrast, the 'Crystal Spine' of 2011 follows Lowell's east-west axis.

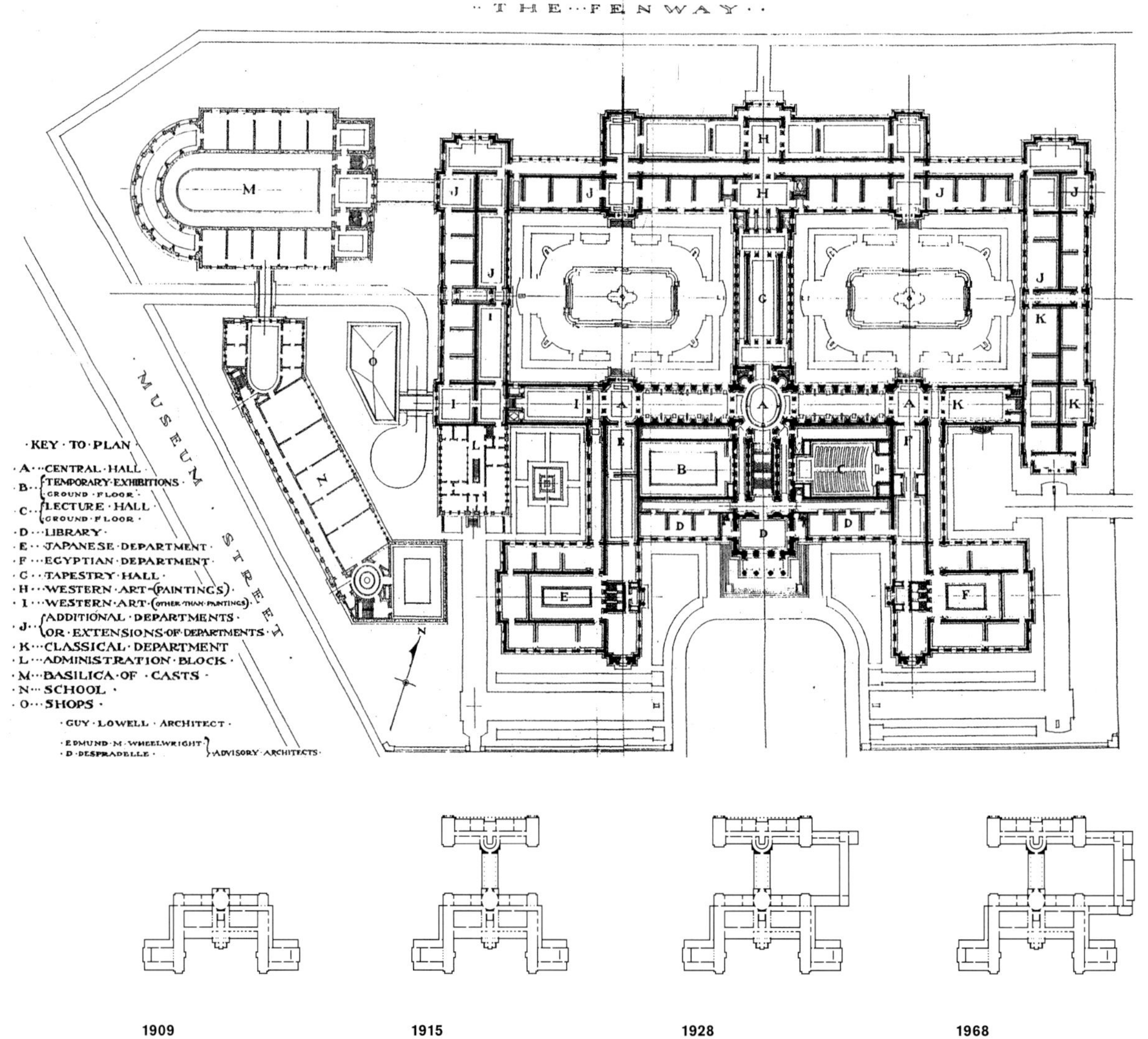

and temperamentally suited to the more than two-decade relationship he would enjoy with the MFA. The scheme he presented in 1907 proposed a Classical 'temple of art', monumental within its park-like surroundings. Two broad wings to the north and south – facing the Back Bay Fens and Huntington Avenue respectively – were linked via a processional north-south axial structure.

Visitors entered either through a monumental portico addressing Huntington Avenue or from the Fenway, where an imposing Ionic colonnade reflected majestically in a broad, lake-like section of the Muddy River, which flows through the Fens. Both north and south entrances led to the double-height Rotunda at the heart of the museum, from which lateral galleries could also be accessed. Secondary east-west axes provided circulation routes through galleries meant to look out on to, and draw natural light from, a balancing pair of courtyard gardens.

The MFA's stately South Wing was the first and largest to be built, at 220,878 square feet (20,520 square metres). The facade of dressed Deer Isle granite, from Maine, extended its symmetrical arms to embrace a recessed entry court along Huntington Avenue. Galleries were arranged according to curatorial discipline – 'a group of museums under one roof', observed the chairman of the MFA trustees at the time. That idea would be recapitulated by the Foster team as they recognised the need to define five 'mini-museums' within the building.

Following completion of the South Wing, a civic-minded patron, Mrs Robert Dawson Evans, offered to fund the entire second phase – the North Wing and link building – as a memorial to her husband. When completed in 1915 it housed a paintings gallery, lecture hall and tapestry gallery, and fully established the museum's major north-south axis. In 1916 John Singer Sargent was commissioned to paint the spectacular murals in the Rotunda and adjoining grand staircase, the last of which were unveiled in 1925, shortly after his death.

Following the construction of the School of the Museum of Fine Arts in 1927, on an adjacent lot to the west, the MFA's trustees proceeded with construction of the Lowell-designed Decorative Arts Wing, a 67,500-square-foot (6,270-square-metre), U-shaped extension to the main building that extended the circulation route to the east, beyond the ends of the North and South Wings. This new building contained galleries and a suite of period rooms and enclosed the East Courtyard and sculpture garden. At this stage in the museum's development, Lowell's 1907 vision had

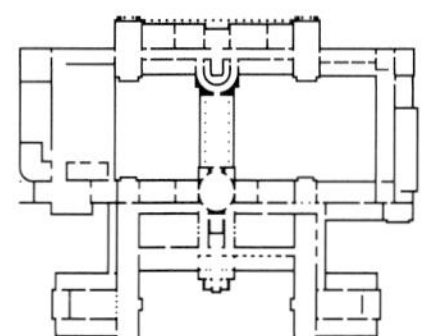

1981

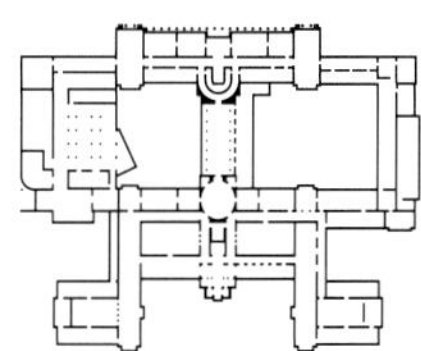

1999

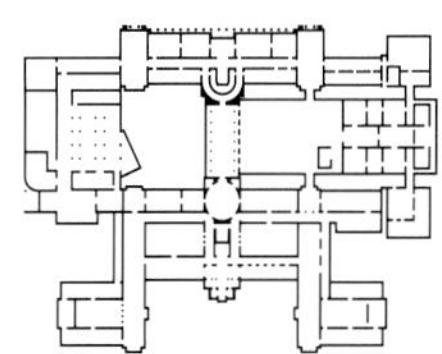

2011

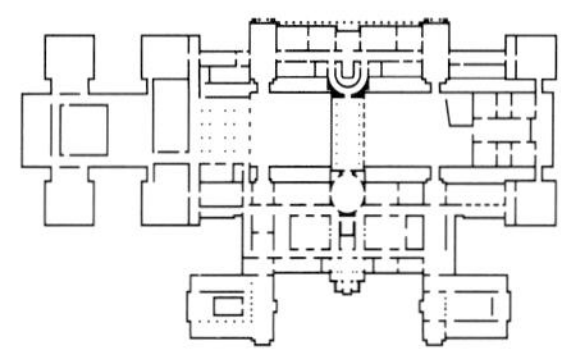

Future

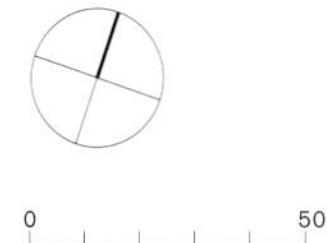

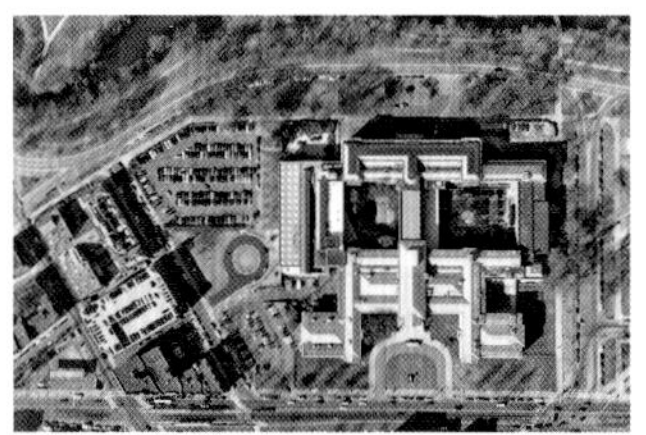

Left: An aerial view of the MFA, circa 1999. IM Pei's West Wing, completed in 1981, became in effect the museum's principal entrance, thus shifting visitor circulation too far to the west.

been adhered to faithfully. Another four decades would pass – through the Great Depression, World War II, and beyond – before further construction took place.

In 1968, the need to house the Forsyth Wickes collection prompted the expansion of the Decorative Arts Wing. Two years later the George Robert White Wing was built to house research and education facilities, a library, dining facilities and administrative offices. Because the White Wing did not replicate the U-shaped footprint of its conceptual twin – the Decorative Arts Wing to the east – the rectangular area envisioned for the second of Lowell's courtyard gardens was truncated. Between 1970 and 1999 a total of 53,160 square feet (4,940 square metres) of Lowell's courtyards was filled in.

By far the most dramatic intervention was IM Pei's West Wing, opened in 1981, which established its own internal logic. By this point, the museum had become a frustrating labyrinth for visitors, full of navigational obstacles. The clear axial routes and vistas that Lowell anticipated had been lost; and the northern entrance from the Fenway and the parkland of the Fens had been closed, effectively capping Lowell's processional north-south axis. Closure of the Fenway Entrance also meant that the museum lost its link with the very parkland with which it was designed to engage. Additionally, because visitor car parking was concentrated in the west, the West Wing eclipsed the Huntington Avenue Entrance as the main point of entry to the museum. In 1990, lack of use led to this historic entrance being closed altogether as a cost-saving measure – an act that Malcolm Rogers, who became the Ann and Graham Gund Director of the MFA in 1994, lamented as signalling 'an abandonment of hope.'

It was Malcolm Rogers who gave energy to the mission to sweep away the museum's staid image and make the institution more accessible – literally and figuratively – to a broader public. Accepting that it might be controversial, on becoming director he reorganised curatorial departments, arranged unprecedented loans and mounted engaging new exhibitions, all calculated to make the museum more approachable through more original and accessible programming. He also felt that too many of the museum's incredible objects languished unseen, vowing to bring objects out of storage and to use them.

Rogers commissioned a new strategic plan, which concluded that the MFA must, among other objectives, improve the care and quality of the collection, enhance the visitor experience, and establish funding for enlarging and upgrading the physical plant to serve

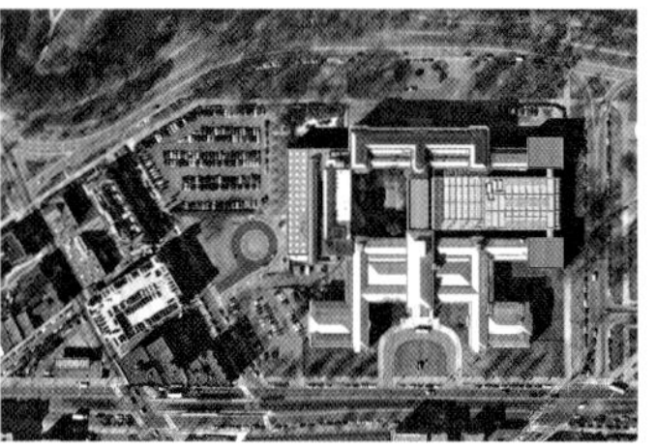

Far left and left: Aerial views of the MFA showing the Shapiro Family Courtyard and the Art of the Americas Wing, completed in 2010; and a corresponding view showing the 'Crystal Spine' masterplan proposals in their entirety, including the Study Centre to the west.

Above: An early visualisation exploring the impact of the 'Crystal Spine' along the MFA's east-west axis. The height of the extension is set lower than the datum of the historic buildings to reduce its visual impact.

Above: Restored and remodelled after three decades of closure, the State Street Corporation Fenway Entrance opens on to the landscape of the Back Bay Fens. It is flanked by Antonio López García's bronze baby heads *Day* and *Night* (2008).

The MFA project looks beyond the confines of a great cultural institution to become the catalyst for the renewal of an entire Boston neighbourhood.
Norman Foster, 2012

Left: The State Street Corporation Fenway Entrance lobby has a new back-painted glass ticketing desk and the original staircase leading up to the Hemicycle has been restored.

the collection and visitors. In March 1999, because of the practice's reputation for working with historic buildings and its deep understanding of how best to present the museum's great works of art, Foster + Partners was appointed to undertake this plan. A new future for the MFA had begun.

Over the next five years, following an analysis of the museum's needs, the design team evaluated a series of masterplanning options before settling on what became known as the 'Crystal Spine'. That scheme stemmed from a recognition that past building campaigns – eight phases over as many decades – had left the visitor experience out of balance with the museum's exhibitions, particularly at the eastern extremities where the public would overlook displays due to the effort involved in finding galleries so distant from visitor parking on the west. Through intensive collaborative study, a holistic solution emerged for the redesign of entry points and circulation routes within the museum, and visitor access and landscaping outside. In addition to endorsing the decision to re-open the Huntington Avenue Entrance – one of Malcolm Rogers' first acts on becoming director – Foster recommended reopening the Fenway Entrance to re-establish the key north-south axis and reclaim the circulation logic of Lowell's plan.

In consultation with the Boston Landmarks Commission, the Foster team undertook the renovation of the north entrance, allowing universal accessibility and introducing granite walkways and sidewalks as part of a comprehensive scheme that fully embraces its parkland context; in 2008 it reopened as the State Street Corporation Fenway Entrance. A similar renovation programme was undertaken for the Huntington Avenue Entrance, which now enjoys dramatically greater use.

Reinforcing the connection with the Back Bay Fens was an essential first step in re-establishing the MFA as a museum 'in the park' rather than merely a museum 'by a park'. The new external landscape elements – designed in collaboration with Kathryn Gustafson – make the transition to the Fens and resonate in turn with the visitor's experience within the museum, where views of green space continue with planting between the new buildings and the historic structures. These green corridors, or 'finger gardens', also provide locations for sculpture and can be glimpsed from outside the museum, creating an invitation to the public to come in and explore. Indeed, the landscaping of the MFA both inside and out has helped fundamentally to promote the museum's connection to Boston's public realm.

Right: The Huntington Avenue Entrance is marked by Thomas Crawford's *Orpheus and Cerberus* (1843). The entrance hall is laid with Tennessee marble. Furniture by designer Florence Knoll is used here and throughout the museum.

Above: Guy Lowell's original Huntington Avenue Entrance was restored and made fully accessible; and the museum's formal north-south circulation axis reinstated.

Above: Sargent's murals for the grand Huntington Avenue staircase include twelve paintings and six reliefs, which depict figures from Classical antiquity: Hercules, Orestes, Apollo and representations of Science, Philosophy and the Unveiling of Truth.

Right: Looking up into the Rotunda. John Singer Sargent's works in this space include eight monumental paintings and twelve reliefs. The performer on the stairs celebrates the opening of the Art of the Americas Wing.

Describing the design team's approach as 'a bold strategy with a light touch', Norman Foster articulated the need to 'integrate and seamlessly meld the old with the new'. With the historic entrances reopened and the north-south axis restored, visitors now access the museum's collections more easily. Indeed, all phases of work, inside and out, have been focused on clear circulation, long vistas and the sequential narrative of the exhibitions.

The design team spent nearly three years studying the museum's collection, identifying its future needs and getting to know all the members of the MFA team – from the director and trustees to the curators of the different departments, conservators and other staff. From that process they developed a strategic overview of the museum and a masterplan for its expansion, which could be delivered in phases as funds allowed.

The idea of having five 'mini-museums' under one roof sprang from an analysis of the collection, which falls into five main curatorial areas: American, Ancient, Asian, Contemporary and European art. The challenge with such a large institution was to make the building more navigable and its collections more comprehensible to the visitor. Organising it into independent pieces – or 'wings' – was identified as a very good way of doing that. The proviso, of course, was that the wings had to fit together to form a clearly legible whole. It is at this point that one begins to appreciate the beauty of the Crystal Spine as a formal device.

The Crystal Spine follows Lowell's long east-west axis – the centre-line of the museum's two large courtyards – to encompass all the new buildings and spaces. The plan anticipated that both of Lowell's external courtyards would be enclosed in crystalline structures – giving the museum the grand public spaces it needed for major events – and that there would be a gradual progression along the spine, from public to semi-public to essentially private functions, beginning with the Art of the Americas Wing in the east and culminating in the MFA school to the far west.

While the Shapiro Family Courtyard and Art of the Americas Wing are the most visible components of the masterplan to date, the project also encompassed significant enhancements to overall circulation, visitor amenities, administrative and storage areas. Behind the scenes, there are new loading docks and secure art paths; mechanical systems throughout the historic sections of the museum have been upgraded; a state-of-the-art energy centre replaces myriad outdated installations; and all the essential servicing infrastructure has been put in place to allow the museum to expand westward in the future.

Left: The Lower Rotunda is the central circulation point of Guy Lowell's north-south axis. Tables with mirrored tops are positioned directly beneath the Rotunda ceiling to highlight John Singer Sargent's murals above.

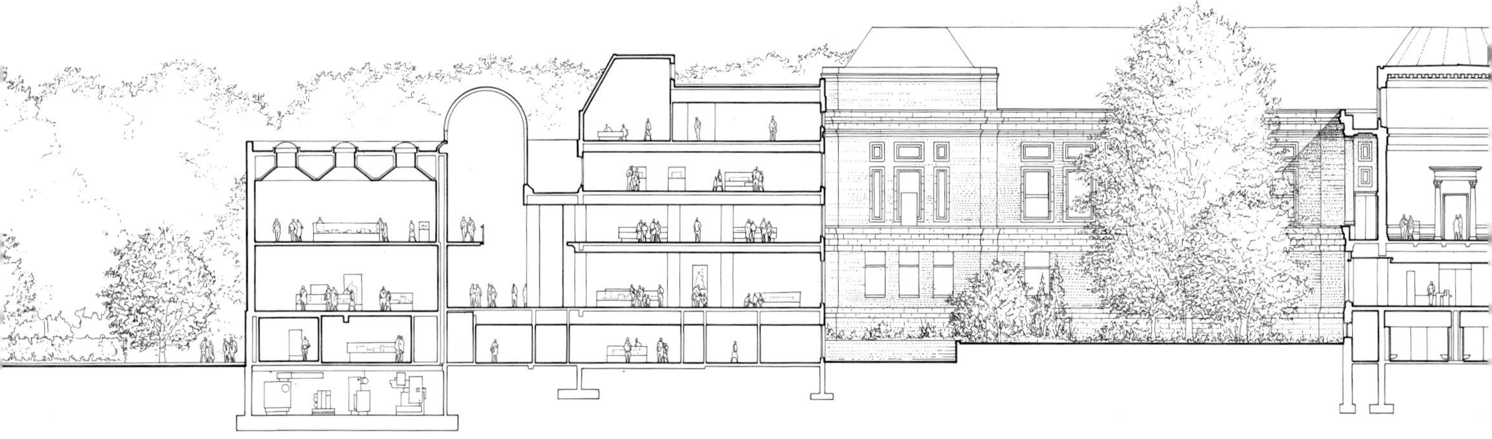

An east-west cross-section through the museum, looking north. Key spaces from left to right are the Linde Family Wing for Contemporary Art; the Calderwood Courtyard; the Shapiro Family Courtyard; and the Art of the Americas Wing.

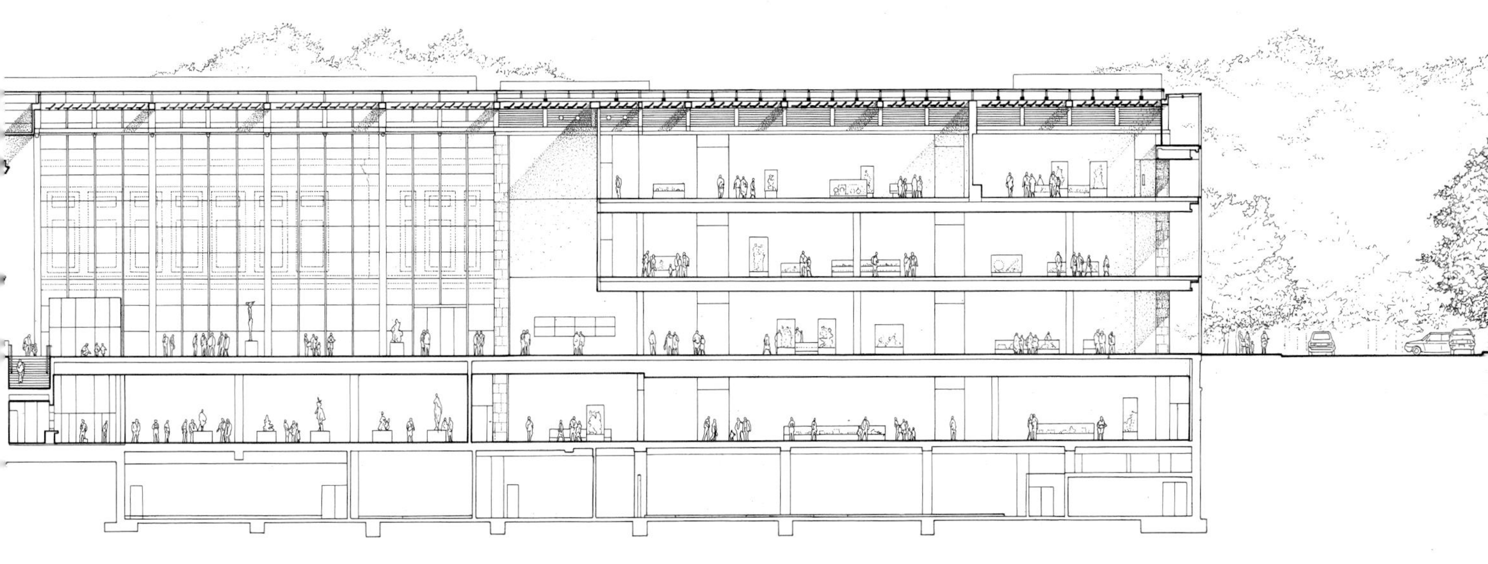

Above: The entrance to the Art of the Americas Wing seen from the Shapiro Family Courtyard. The courtyard contains large sculptural works, such as Zhan Wang's *Artificial Rock #85,* seen here.

Right: The courtyard glazing is engineered to accommodate snow loading and to reduce energy requirements for heating and air conditioning. Acoustic absorbance and a public-address system are incorporated within the columns.

At the heart of the institution the architects have created a lofty space that is flooded with ethereal light. The expanse of the sky and the greenery of the parkland are brought into the museum. Edwin Heathcote, *Financial Times*, 20 November 2010

Above: Translucent hinged ceiling panels in the Shapiro Family Courtyard admit diffused daylight and provide sun shading. The panels can be back-lit to animate the space for evening performances and gala events.

The Art of the Americas Wing is a deeply humane, deeply thoughtful piece of architecture. Robert Campbell, *The Boston Globe*, 20 November 2010

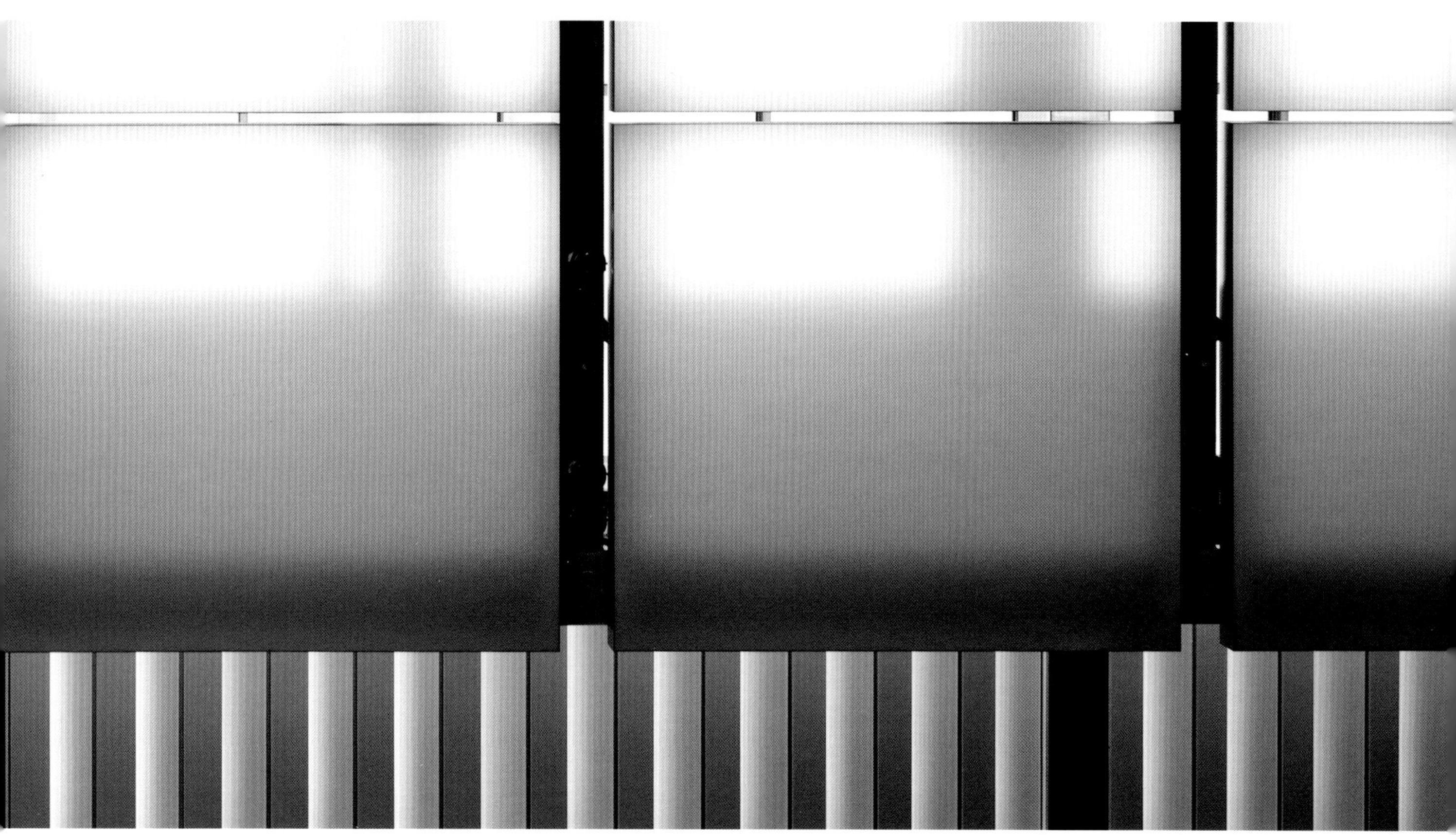

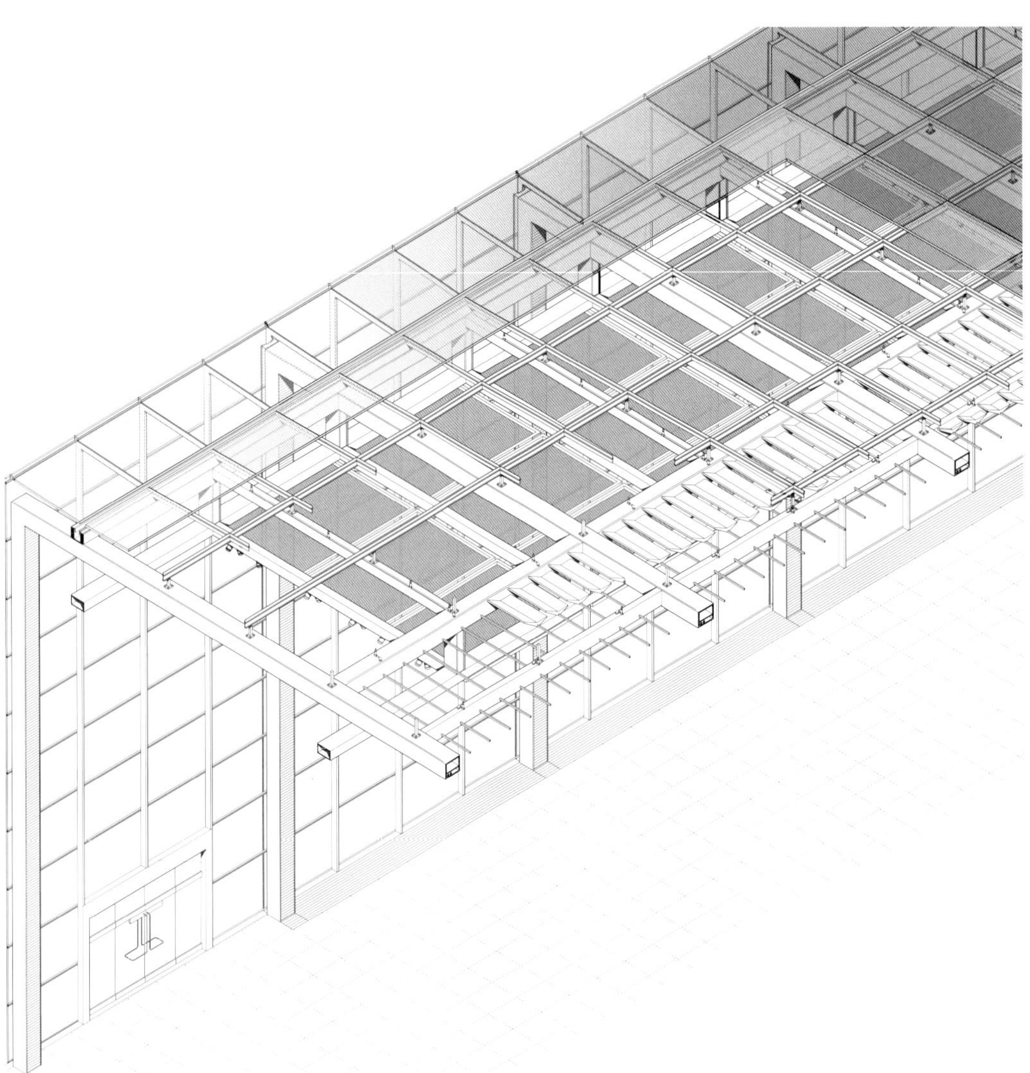

Above: A cutaway drawing of the courtyard structure and roof glazing.

Right: Looking up at the courtyard ceiling, which incorporates translucent screens for sun shading.

ART OF THE
AMERICAS
RUTH AND CARL J. SHAPIRO
COURTYARD

Left: Looking into the Art of the Americas Wing. The collection is organised chronologically, the period represented on each level being indicated by strategically placed objects and works of art.

Above: The Shapiro Family Courtyard is a social focal point within the museum. It is a place for visitors to meet and relax, and a venue for group activities.

Right: Film screenings, concerts and lectures are held in the 150-seat Barbara and Theodore Alfond Auditorium on Level LG.

With the basic elements of the masterplan in place, the curatorial challenge was to ensure a coherent transition between the different 'wings'. That involved the architects working closely with Malcolm Rogers and his curators to determine how the collection would be arranged gallery by gallery, floor by floor. It also suggested that each collection should have its own 'front door', ideally accessed directly from a space on the Crystal Spine. The masterplan allows each of the five wings to be entered from one of the two courtyards. From the Shapiro Family Courtyard, visitors can enter the renovated Art of Europe galleries to the north, or the Art of the Ancient World galleries to the south, and the new galleries in the Art of the Americas Wing to the east.

Throughout the building, signage is kept to a minimum – a strategy that works because the circulation routes that Foster has established are essentially intuitive. Each of the three main collection 'entrances' within the courtyard is signposted by a large, representative work of art, which beckons you in; similarly, within the galleries as you move around your eye is drawn to a significant object in an adjacent space, which offers another visual cue.

Although the Art of the Americas Wing represents only the first phase of the museum's expansion, it has already become its cultural centrepiece. The new wing adds fifty-three galleries for the display of more than 5,000 objects from the museum's American collections – twice as many as previously on view – and increases the building's total area by 28 per cent. From the courtyard, a cantilevered staircase offers glimpses into the three above-ground gallery floors. The staircase projects into the courtyard, its landings providing vantage points as visitors move from level to level. Natural light floods in, giving the courtyard the airy transparency of an outdoor social plaza.

The courtyard is where visitors can meet friends, plan their museum visit, lunch at the popular New American Café, or progress into the adjacent galleries. At the western end of the space, a lift and staircase lead down to the Ann and Graham Gund Gallery for special exhibitions, a flexible space designed with moveable walls and leading-edge lighting to serve temporary exhibitions of varying scope and media. This gallery is significant in that it not only provides the museum with an adaptable space for the display of travelling and temporary exhibitions, but its completion freed the West Wing of this role. Now renamed the Linde Family Wing for Contemporary Art, it has been transformed to house the MFA's Contemporary Art collection – the final piece in the jigsaw.

Left: The Sharf Visitor Center on Level 1 is located in the heart of the museum, on the main north-south axis. It is a place to meet friends or gather for a tour.

Above: *Fresh Ink: Ten Takes on Chinese Tradition*, was the inaugural exhibition in the Ann and Graham Gund Gallery for temporary exhibitions on Level LG.

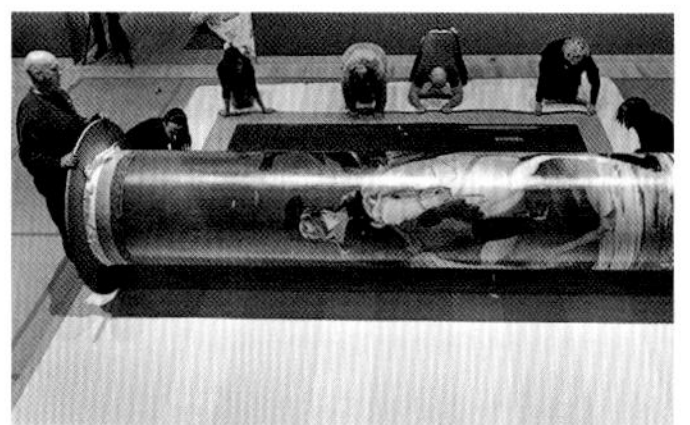

Left: Thomas Sully's monumental canvas, *The Passage of the Delaware* (1819) is unrolled, prior to framing. Too large to be hung in any of the museum's historic galleries, the painting had languished in storage for many years.

At the western end of the Shapiro Family Courtyard, the existing brick wall of Lowell's link building stands as a rustic foil to the smooth walls of ivory-coloured French Crema Luna limestone that introduce the Art of the Americas Wing to the east. The paving is Kuru Grey granite from Finland. While beautiful, the highly sound-reflective granite and glass surfaces of the courtyard presented a serious acoustic challenge. The project team sought a relatively quiet and 'contemplative' baseline environment despite the anticipated presence of hundreds of visitors in motion as well as a busy café.

In addition, the courtyard needed to function as the museum's primary venue for large ceremonial and social events, when appropriate reverberation rates for amplified speech and music are critical. A superior sound-absorption coefficient was achieved for the space by placing acoustic material in the ceiling's central band of V-shaped baffles, which also control heat gain and glare. Adding glass fibres to the inside of the columns that contain public address speakers further reduced reverberation, as did the wooden fins affixed to the west wall. In this way a bare minimum of aesthetic intrusion was required for acoustic control.

The new wing consists of a central, axial structure flanked by two almost symmetrical pavilions, linked to it on the north and south by glazed 'bridges'. Beyond the bridges lie the planted sculpture gardens, which run between the courtyard and the historic buildings. These garden spaces not only create a sense of continuity with the surrounding greenery, but also accommodate seismic events by serving as buffer zones allowing new buildings to move independent of the old ones in the event of an earthquake.

Boston lies in a seismic zone – a huge swathe of the city was damaged in the Cape Ann quake of 1755 and minor tremors have hit the area since – and the historic museum buildings are not seismic compliant. Modern codes demanded that either the entire building had to be upgraded or the new work needed to be articulated as a seismically rated independent structure. The 20-foot (6-metre) depth of the gardens allows the two buildings to move independently during an earthquake, so that one can shift without damaging the other. Seismic joints also articulate the transitions between new and old construction, but overall the courtyard reads as a freestanding glass object surrounded by the museum's existing buildings and new galleries.

Exterior glazing on the new wing's central building, bridges, and other components gives a high degree of transparency, making the MFA feel more accessible

Right: Seen here newly installed, *The Passage of the Delaware* serves as a focal point of the Arts of the New Nation gallery on Level 1, which is dedicated to the iconography of the new nation immediately after the American Revolution.

Right: Works are installed in The Salon: Americans Abroad in the Nineteenth Century on Level 2. Sculptures by William Wetmore Story, Harriet Hosmer, Horatio Greenough, and other artists active in Rome, illustrate American achievement in the mid-nineteenth century.

and inviting. From outside, passers-by can see gallery visitors viewing sculpture in perimeter passageways and traversing connector bridges, giving a sense of the life within the museum. Inside, visitors can appreciate a generous measure of natural light – a rarity in museum settings – and they can enjoy new vistas of Boston, from Fenway Park to Back Bay and beyond.

While the design of the Art of the Americas wing is manifestly modern, its materials and scale nonetheless present rich contextual sympathies with the museum's adjacent historic structures. Stone cladding on the North and South Pavilions is the same Deer Isle granite, quarried in Maine, used for the museum's original 1909 building, creating continuity with the architectural legacy of Lowell.

Inside the museum the design team also respected context in the transitions from gallery to gallery, from one curatorial focus to another. 'The focus was very much on the works of art: we wanted the architectural experience to play a supporting role', says Spencer de Grey. That ambition has certainly been met – the art and its display draw visitors through the new spaces in a compelling manner. Arranged along the central spine of the plan on four levels, the core galleries are designated for the larger, more iconic works while the flanking galleries and the North and South Pavilions are partitioned to feature art-historical periods, themes and concentrated presentations of single arts. These can include diverse media, from painting and sculpture to furniture, ceramics, stained glass, textiles and other decorative arts. Shaded lancet windows allow indirect natural light into side gallery spaces from the sculpture gardens.

To find the earliest works from the MFA's collection – ancient art of the Americas, early Native American art, seventeenth-century works, and maritime arts – one descends from the courtyard to the lower-ground level. Here, an outstanding collection of ancient South and Central American art includes textiles from Peru, worked gold objects from Costa Rica, Colombia and Panama, Olmec jades, decorated burial urns, and an array of ancient musical instruments: ocarinas, shell trumpets, drums and rattles. Ship models and related maritime arts are displayed in an exquisite side gallery that celebrates the golden age of ship-building, with models of historic vessels such as the frigate USS *Constitution* and the clipper *Flying Cloud*. It is here that the beautifully detailed display cabinets are best appreciated. With their minimalist components, undetectable hardware, and clean connections between base and glass, they essentially disappear in the presence of the works of art.

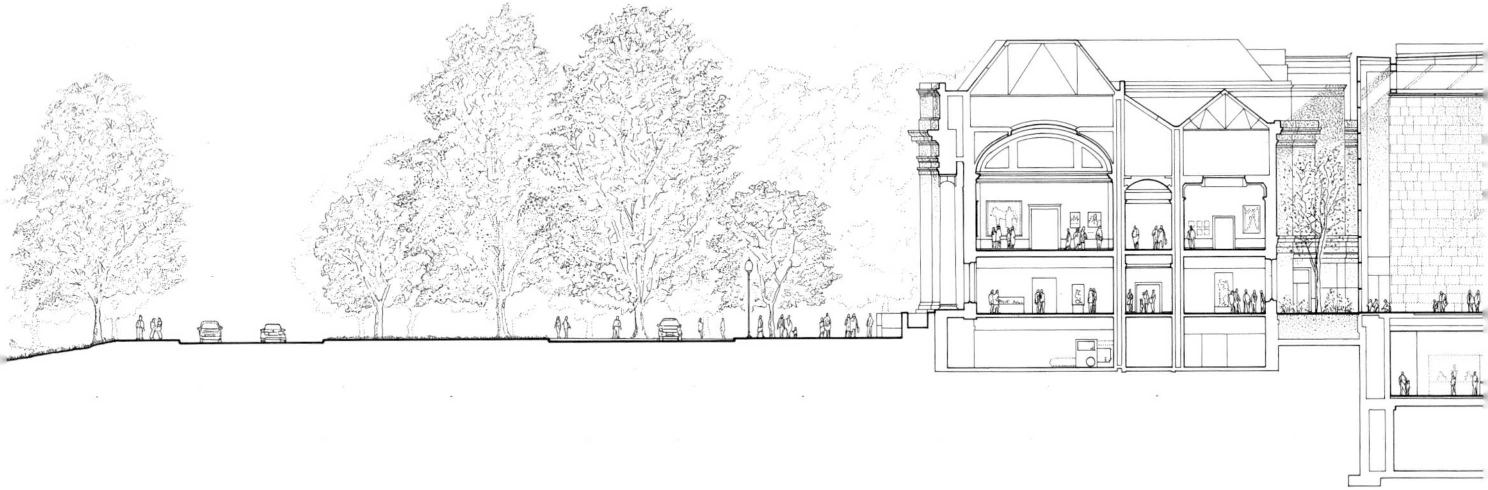

A north-south cross-section through the Shapiro Family Courtyard, looking east towards the entrance to the Art of the Americas Wing. To the left is Guy Lowell's original Art of Europe Wing; to the right is the Art of the Ancient World Wing.

Above: Landscaped 'finger' gardens to the north and south of the courtyard create a visual link to the greenery of the Back Bay Fens and provide display space for sculpture from the collection. Seen here is *Hermes Resting on a Rock*, viewed from the Art of the Ancient World wing.

Right: The gardens also provide seismic separation from the historic museum buildings – an essential consideration in Boston.

The glass walls of the courtyard establish a minimal boundary with the exterior, allowing for an intimate connection to the surrounding greenery and the protective embrace of the Beaux-Arts edifice. David Galbraith, *Architizer*, 15 November 2010

Left: Opening celebrations for the Art of the Americas Wing, held in the Shapiro Family Courtyard, 12 November 2010.

Level 1, corresponding with the museum's principal level, houses eighteenth-century art of the colonial Americas and early-nineteenth-century art, which is most visitors' first encounter with the MFA's new Americas narrative. Chief among its spectacular objects is Paul Revere's famous work in silver, *The Sons of Liberty Bowl* (1768), which occupies a dedicated cabinet in the Colonial Boston gallery. The Foster team worked closely with curators to tailor the exhibition spaces to specific objects in the collection, such as this. The Goppion Museum Workshop of Milan manufactured more than 200 climate-controlled display cases, designed for particular objects or for flexible future use.

Nearby hangs John Singleton Copley's iconic portrait of Revere, the patriot-silversmith, one of many intuitive placements of two-dimensional art with three-dimensional objects. Special consideration was given to accommodating outsized works, such as *The Passage of the Delaware*, by Thomas Sully (1819), which hangs in the adjacent Arts of the New Nation gallery. This monumental painting, which depicts George Washington about to cross the Delaware on Christmas night 1776, before surprising British troops at Trenton, is the anchor for the entire first level and sets the revolutionary tone of the works represented.

Other key art works are placed strategically to draw visitors into the theme of a particular era. Not far from General Washington hangs Miguel Cabrera's portrait *Don Manuel Jose Rubio y Salinas, Archbishop of Mexico* (1754), a recent acquisition, which serves as a focal point of the gallery New Spain and the Spanish Tradition, where Peruvian tapestries and a range of decorative arts tell a parallel colonial story. Throughout the wing, great care was taken to exhibit pieces to best advantage and with due regard to context. Historically researched paint colours and era-specific textiles and wallpapers were carefully chosen to resonate with the works of art in their respective galleries. Decorative arts are mounted on low plinths, which constitute the objects' own framing devices, and flooring of American red oak from the Pacific Northwest provides a point of continuity throughout.

Ascending through the 'floating' staircase, visitors arrive at Level 2, which features nineteenth-century and early twentieth-century art. This section begins with a stunning display of the work of expatriate painter John Singer Sargent, who lived abroad for most of his life but retained US citizenship. The gallery is dominated by Sargent's charming and enigmatic *The Daughters of Edward Darley Boit* (1882), painted in Paris and exhibited at the Salon of 1883. In this

Right: The courtyard can accommodate a range of gala and fundraising events; its character changes dramatically after dark.

unusual portrait, the four Boit girls are seen as if caught in play, one of them standing in the shadows against one of a pair of larger-than-life Japanese ceramic vases. Astonishingly, in the gallery, the canvas is flanked by the vases depicted in the painting. The curators' vision in juxtaposing Japanese decorative arts with an American painting (created in Paris) in such an appropriate way as to seem intuitive exemplifies the refreshing departure that the MFA has made from the dry typological and thematic march that one experiences in most museums.

The Foster team encouraged such creative possibilities by designing gallery spaces with framing devices and cabinets that incorporate clear and non-reflective glass to allow decorative arts to be juxtaposed with paintings and works in a multitude of other media. Following Sargent, the Level 2 galleries illustrate great American genre and landscape painting of the nineteenth century, at home and abroad. Once again, paintings combine with decorative arts, primarily in thematic side galleries, to enliven the discussion of key periods: Gothic Revival is highlighted with furniture by Joseph Meeks and landscape paintings by artists of the Hudson River School; the Aesthetic Movement is illuminated by the American art glass of Louis Comfort Tiffany and John LaFarge and paintings by William Merritt Chase and James Abbott MacNeill Whistler; and the high points of the American Arts and Crafts Movement are represented by furniture designed by Frank Lloyd Wright and Gustav Stickley. Folk Art has its dedicated gallery, with simple portraits of children, weather vanes, quilts, and charming animal sculptures.

Two period rooms – the Roswell Gleason parlor and dining room – are assembled for the first time since they were acquired by the MFA in 1977. While period rooms have fallen out of favour in many museums, the MFA has made the bold decision to amplify this aspect of its collection by incorporating nine rooms – dating from the early 1700s to the mid-1800s – into the new wing. To make the viewing experience as authentic as possible, the positions of period windows were accommodated in the design of the exterior fenestration so that natural light flows into the rooms as it would have done originally. From the outside, one can 'read' the presence of the period rooms in the asymmetrical placement of window openings.

While lower-level gallery spaces enjoy a generous height of nearly 16 feet (4.88 metres), Level 3's core galleries – positioned at the top of the central spine of the new buildings – rise to nearly 22 feet (6.7 metres) to accommodate monumental twentieth-century

Right: The Shapiro Family Courtyard has given the museum the flexible reception space it required. It is seen here hosting a formal luncheon for sponsors.

paintings and sculpture. Side galleries feature painting, sculpture, jewellery and other media created through the mid-1990s. Colour Field painting, Abstract Expressionism, Minimalism and related movements are featured on this level, along with photography. Also featured are examples from the museum's growing collection of Latin American art, such as Argentinian César Paternosto's *Staccato* (1965), which resonates with American works by Josef Albers and Stuart Davis. The twentieth century represents the MFA's most promising opportunity for growth and these spaces were designed to accept the wide range of modern and contemporary art, yet to be acquired. As in the Shapiro Family Courtyard, louvred panels filter natural light transmitted through a glazed ceiling.

Four 'behind the scenes' galleries, with the themes Collecting, Classifying, Curating and Conserving, are located at the eastern end of Levels 1 and 2, where views of the city provide a backdrop for study stations at which visitors may learn more about objects, their eras and styles. Conservation techniques are also interpreted, using objects from the collections to demonstrate ways in which works of art are prepared for exhibition. At the eastern end of Level 3 is the trustees' meeting room; office space is located in the North and South Pavilions at Levels 3 and 4. Accessible from ground level is a 150-seat auditorium for lectures, concerts and films. Adjacent to the auditorium are two studio-art classrooms and a seminar room.

Beyond the new exhibition and public spaces is a further 70,000 square feet (6,500 square metres) of gallery renovations and below-grade expansion to serve the museum's administrative, conservation, storage and mechanical needs. Environmental concerns were systematically addressed throughout, both in the historic building and the new wing. Improvements within existing structures have boosted the museum's overall energy efficiency by 10 per cent. Triple glazing in the new wing minimises heat gain, thereby reducing the need for mechanical ventilation; and a carefully conceived lighting plan employs natural light wherever possible to reduce demand for artificial illumination.

In 2011 the Royal Institute of British Architects awarded the Museum of Fine Arts, Boston project an International Award for architectural excellence. While the renovation and expansion at the MFA meets the goals that Foster, the MFA trustees, and the city of Boston discussed and agreed during the years of planning, the success of the bold new 'Crystal Spine' and the dialogue with the museum's historic buildings, comes down to the ability to blend a great institution's identity with its peerless collection and its locale.

Left: Fully accessible, low-level steel-and-glass stands, seen here, provide exhibit information throughout the museum, except for the nine period rooms, which have purpose-designed bronze railings and plaques.

Far left: A recreation of Elizabeth Derby West's master bedchamber at Oak Hill – one of nine period rooms newly installed on Level 1.

Left: The parlor and dining room from the 1840s Roswell Gleason House. The setting includes original woodwork, doors and fireplaces; original pieces include the dining table and chandelier.

Above: The Shepard Parlor – a recreation of the room in George Shepard's 1803 mansion in Maine with original hand-printed French wallpaper. Note the windows rear and right, which match external windows to admit filtered daylight.

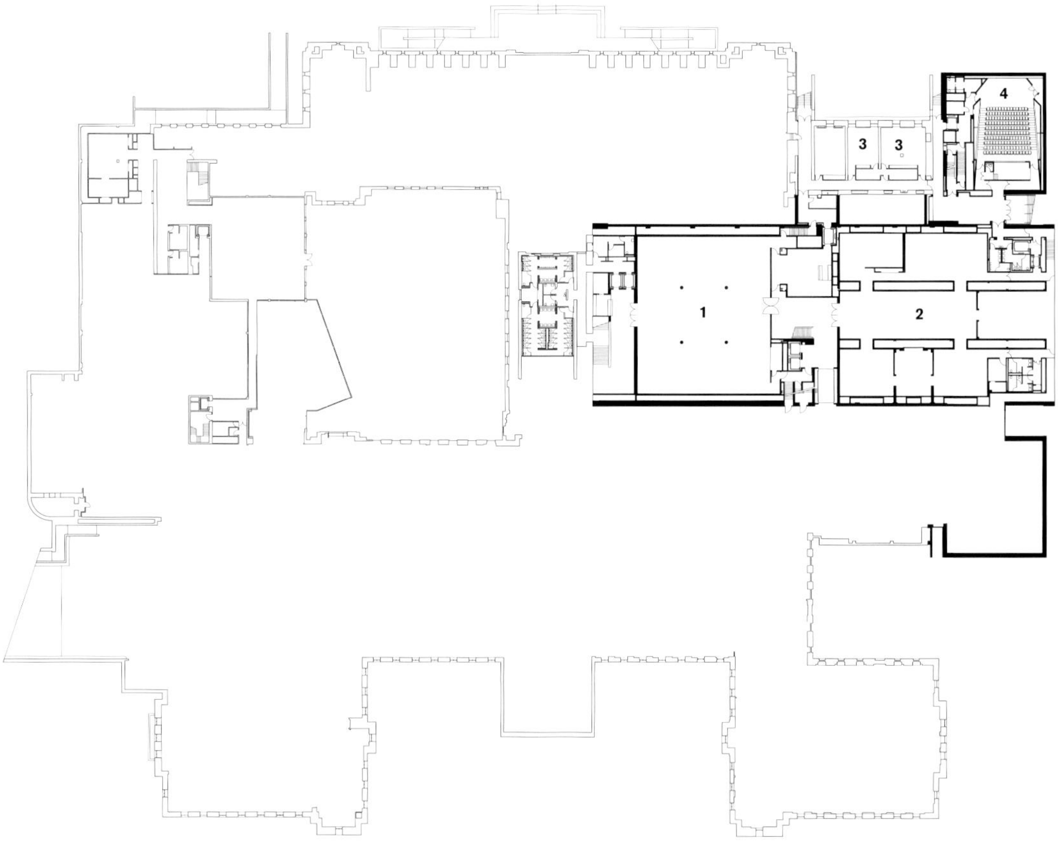

Above: Plan at Level LG.

Right: Plan at Level 1.

1 Gund Gallery for Special Exhibitions
2 Art of the Americas
3 studio art classrooms
4 Alfond Auditorium
5 Linde Family Wing for Contemporary Art
6 Art of Asia, Oceania and Africa
7 Torf Gallery for Special Exhibitions
8 Lower Rotunda
9 Huntington Avenue Entrance
10 Art of the Ancient World
11 Shapiro Family Courtyard
12 Sharf Visitor Center
13 Art of Europe
14 State Street Corporation Fenway Entrance
15 Calderwood Courtyard

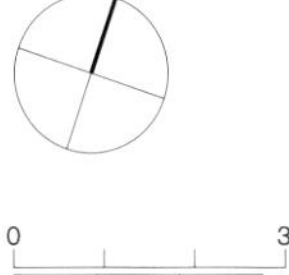

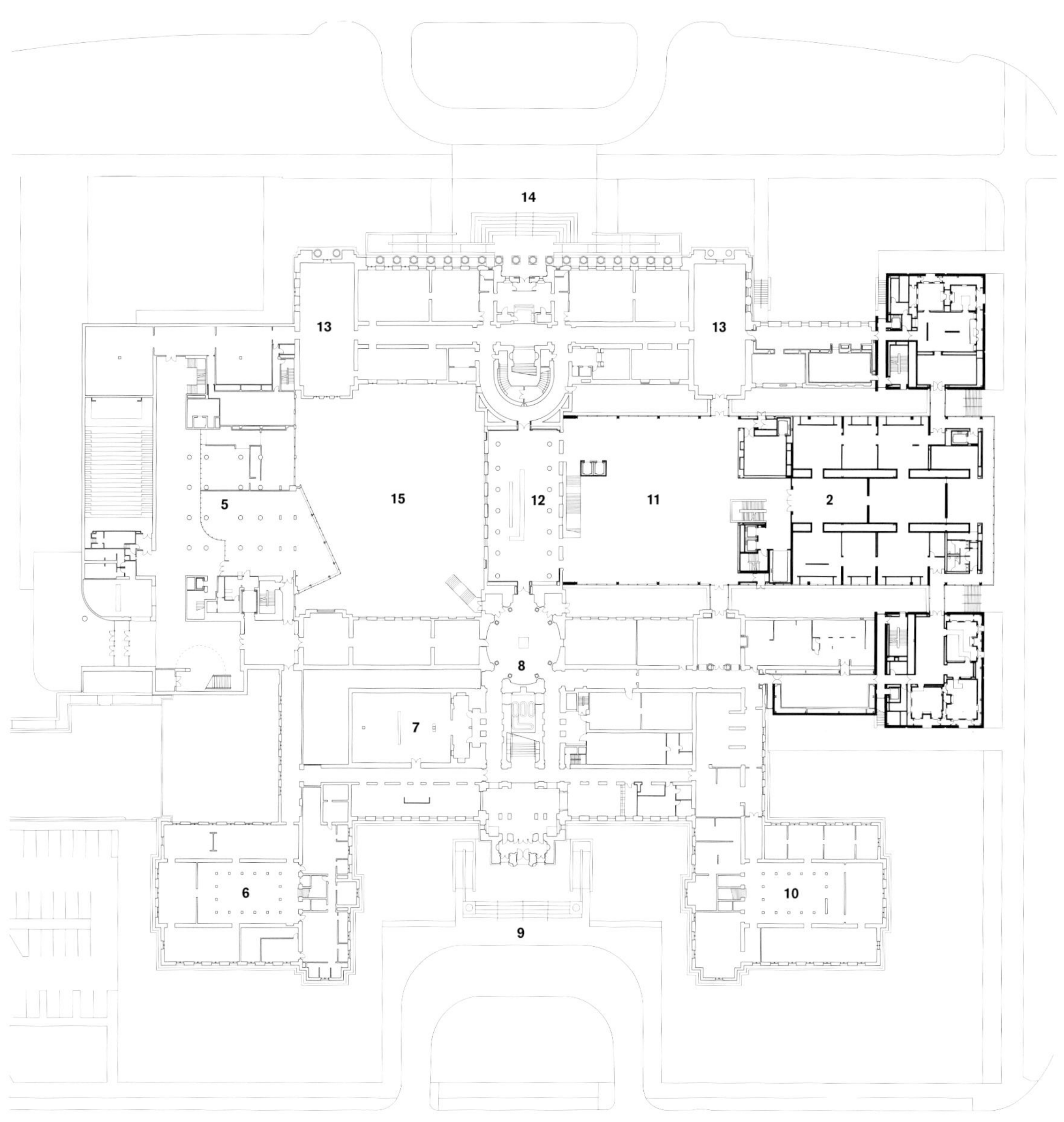
14
13
13
5
15
12
11
2
8
7
6
10
9

BUILDING THE NEW MFA
CAMPAIGN DONORS
ART OF THE
AMERICAS

Left: Looking down into the galleries on Level LG, which contain works from the museum's Ancient American, Native North American and seventeenth-century collections.

Above: Specially designed display cases, made in Italy by Goppion, were created to hold special works, such as the Mayan funerary urns seen here.

Previous pages: The George Putnam Gallery on Level LG features American ship models and maritime art. The Goppion display cases have low-iron glass to minimise reflection and colour distortion.

Left: The Carolyn and Peter Lynch Gallery on Level 1 contains works from colonial-era Boston, including John Singleton Copley's 1768 portrait of revolutionary and silversmith Paul Revere, whose *The Sons of Liberty Bowl* is seen in the foreground.

Above: The east wall of the Lynch Gallery is lined with wallpaper. Backdrops for individual works were chosen to reflect the period and can be altered without affecting the walls or flooring.

One of the things that's unique about the Art of the Americas Wing is that we bring all media together with an intelligent, lively conversation. Malcolm Rogers, Ann and Graham Gund Director, Museum of Fine Arts, Boston, 2010

Left: Standing in the Kristin and Roger Servison Gallery: New Nation 1800-1830 on Level 1, looking through to the Liberty Mutual: American Artists Abroad 1770-1820 gallery. Seen centre is Benjamin West's painting *King Lear*, 1806.

Above: Thomas Sully's monumental painting *The Passage of the Delaware*, 1819, which stands nearly 16.5 feet (5 metres) tall, determined the scale of the Kristin and Roger Servison Gallery on Level 1.

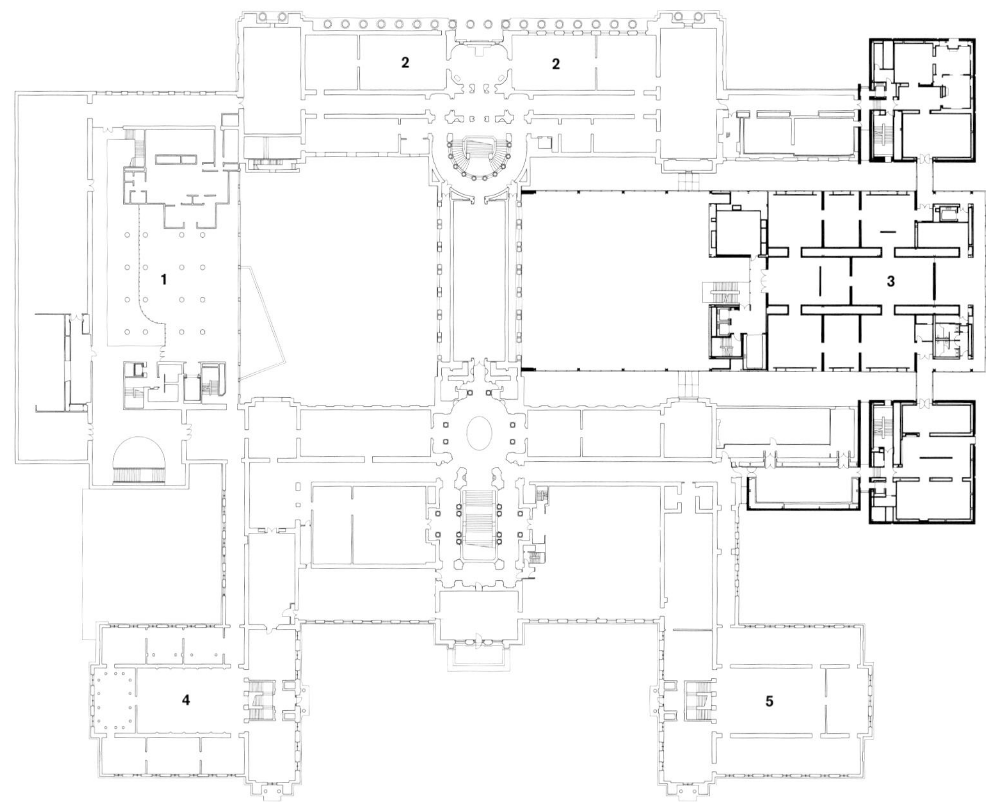

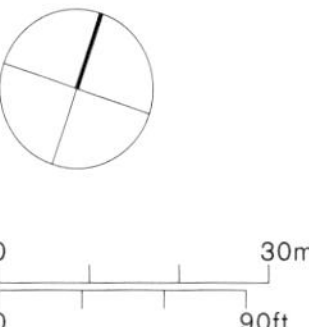

0 30m
0 90ft

Five collections under one roof:

1 Contemporary Art
2 Art of Europe
3 Art of the Americas
4 Art of Asia, Oceania and Africa
5 Art of the Ancient World

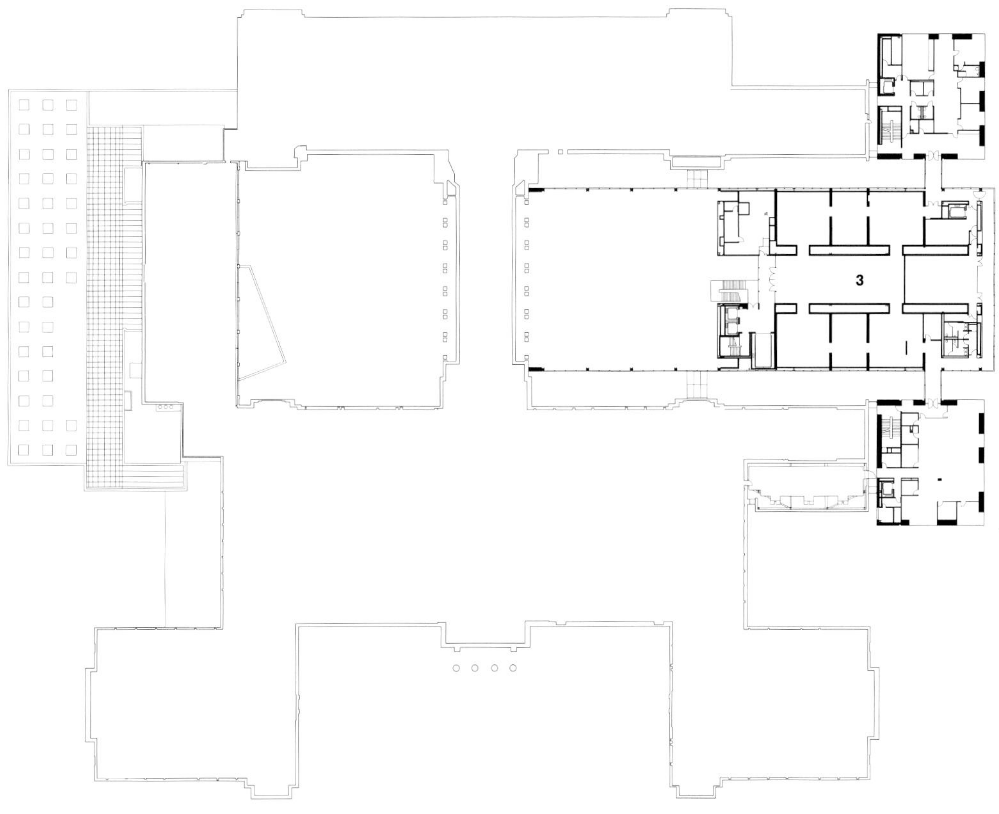

Left: Plan at Level 2.

Above: Plan at Level 3.

PENNY AND JEFF VINIK GALLERY

In a gallery like this, you see the three-dimensional objects talking to the two-dimensional and suddenly the sculptures seem at home. Malcolm Rogers, Ann and Graham Gund Director, Museum of Fine Arts, Boston, 2010

Previous pages: The Salon: Americans Abroad in the Nineteenth Century on Level 2. The gallery is lined with burgundy damask and contains paintings by Americans depicting the New World and Europe hung from high-level picture rails in the style of a salon.

Left: The John Singer Sargent Gallery on Level 2 contains one of Sargent's masterpieces, *The Daughters of Edward Darley Boit*, 1882. Boit family Japanese vases featured in the painting are displayed alongside.

Above: Each of the galleries on Level 2 is differentiated by its wall treatment. Burgundy damask in The Salon contrasts with grey brocade in the John Singer Sargent Gallery. Sargent's portrait of Charles Stewart, Sixth Marquess of Londonderry, 1904, is seen centre.

AN AMERICAN
RENAISSANCE
LORRAINE AND

Previous pages: Frank Duveneck and Clement John Barnhorn's marble *Tomb Effigy of Elizabeth Boott Duveneck*, 1894, is the feature of the Jan and Warren Adelson Gallery: An American Renaissance 1875-1914 on Level 2.

Left: The Lane Collection Gallery on Level 3 contains American Modernist works. Interactive multimedia tables in the gallery allow visitors to research works of art, orientate themselves in the museum, and access visitor information portals.

Above: The John Axelrod Gallery on Level 3 contains American works from the 1920s and '30s. Bespoke Goppion cases contain special works, including Viktor Schreckengost's glazed porcelain punch bowl from his 'Jazz Bowl' series, and displays of couture and decorative art.

Above: Erwin Hauer's screens frame views east from Level 2 of the Art of the Americas Wing. The Prudential Tower and the John Hancock Tower are seen in the distance.

In creating an Art of the Americas Wing and throwing its institutional weight behind the idea, the museum has pushed the study of American art in new directions. Holland Cotter, *New York Times*, 18 November 2010

Although many of the galleries are by definition inward-looking, we wanted to give visitors the feeling that they were in a building that had views. So we devised colonnades on each of the floors, which look out over the Fens.
Spencer de Grey, of Foster + Partners, 2012

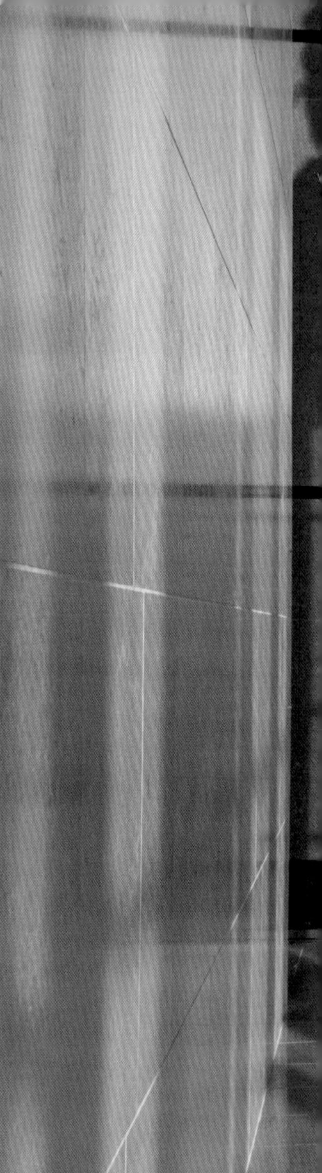

Left: The glazed upper-level walkways in the South and North Pavilions have views across the landscape of the Back Bay Fens and downtown Boston.

Above: Moveable screens designed by the Austrian-American artist, Erwin Hauer, line the eastern facade. The sculpture *Young Diana*, 1923, by Anna Hyatt Huntington stands at the north-east corner on Level 2.

SAUNDRA B. AND WILLIAM H. LANE GALLERIES

EXIT

There's not a white wall to be found, even in the lofty top-floor galleries devoted to modern art. Too often strong wall colours muddy art. Here paintings pop. James S Russell, *Bloomberg Businessweek,* 24 November 2010

Previous pages: The Sandra B and William H Lane Gallery – American Abstraction – on Level 3, which is top-lit with adjustable louvres to control lighting levels.

Left: The 1940s and 1950s Gallery on Level 3 highlights works of American Modernism, including furniture by Charles and Ray Eames.

Above: Looking from the Lane Gallery – American Abstraction – into the Mid-Century Expressionism Gallery, where the focal point is a one-third-scale plaster model of Walter Hancock's Pennsylvania Railroad World War II Memorial, seen at centre.

ART OF THE AMERICAS

ART OF THE AMERICAS

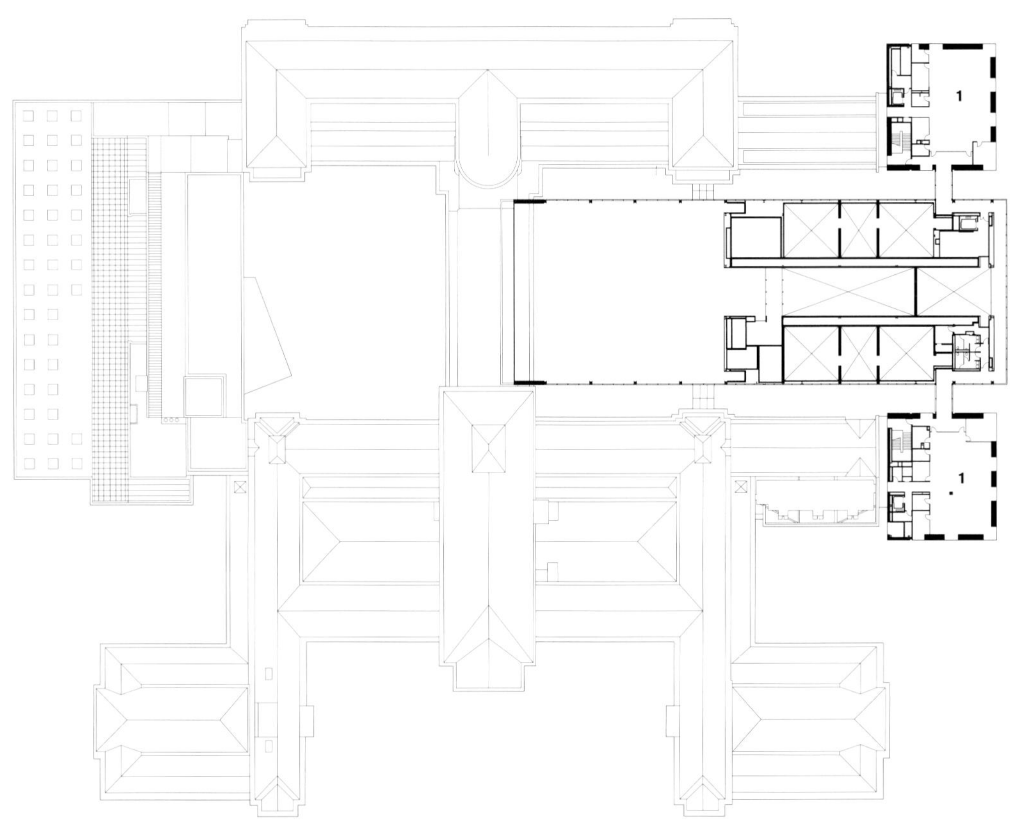

Previous pages: The Lane Gallery – American Abstraction – on Level 3. All the galleries have American red oak flooring. Entrances to connecting galleries have grey granite thresholds and peened stainless-steel panelling.

Above: Plan at Level 4.

Right: Roof plan.

1 administrative offices

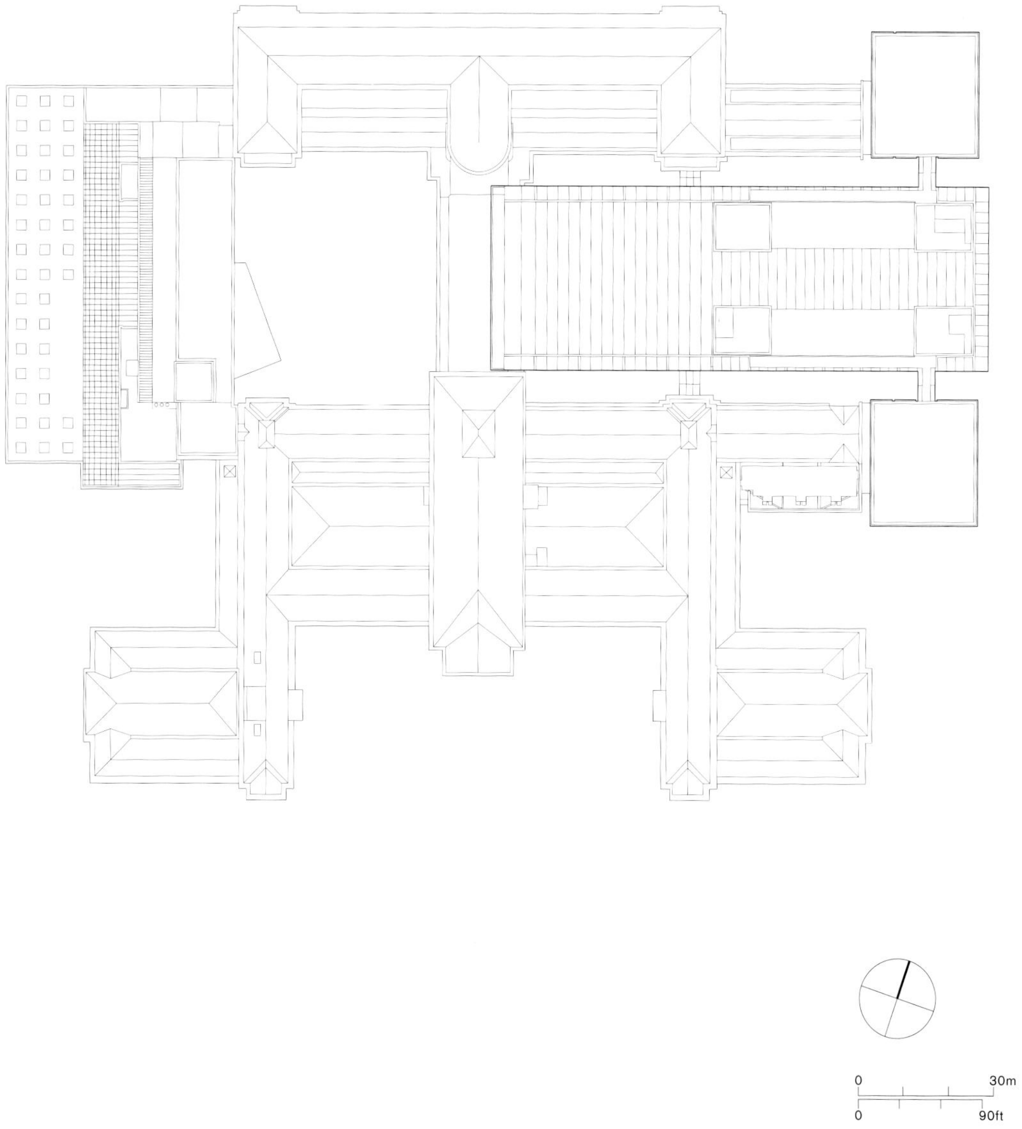

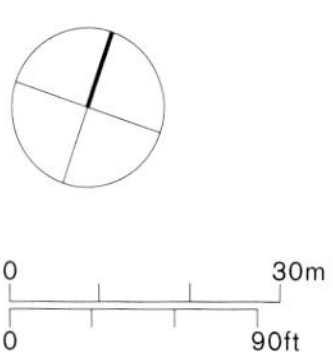
0
30m
0
90ft

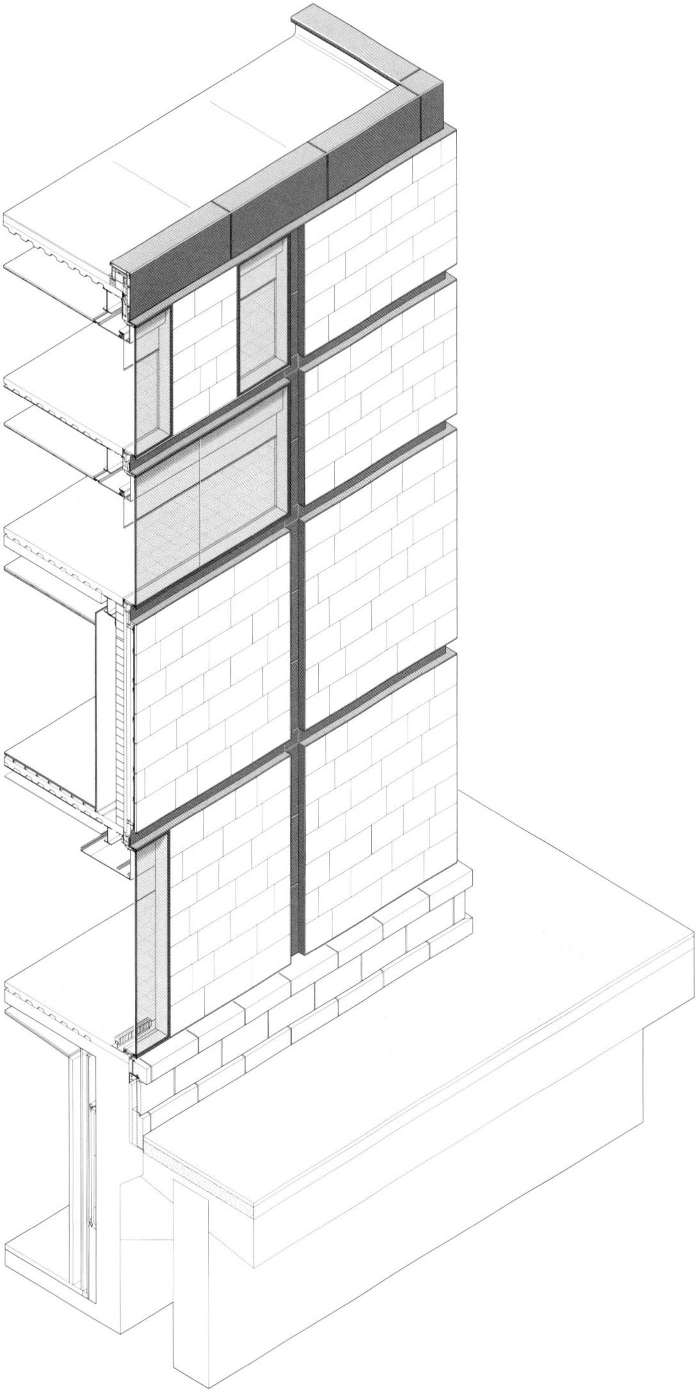

Left: A detail of the South Pavilion of the Art of the Americas Wing.

Right: An axonometric drawing of the facade of the South Pavilion. The Deer Isle granite cladding is the same as that used for the original museum buildings.

Above: The eastern facade of the Art of the Americas Wing expresses the interior arrangement of galleries, with glazing matching fenestration in period rooms and vertical channels indicating walls.

Right: Animated by sculpture and Erwin Hauer's moveable screens, the glass walkways along the eastern facade of Art of the Americas Wing link to the North and South Pavilions and provide visitors with places to pause and enjoy the view.

Above: A detail of Guy Lowell's Robert Dawson Evans Wing of 1915, with its Ionic columns, with the North Pavilion of the Art of the Americas Wing beyond.

Right: The Fenway Entrance seen from the east. The approach from the Back Bay Fens has been remodelled and re-landscaped and is now fully accessible. Antonio López García's bronze heads *Day* and *Night* frame the entrance.

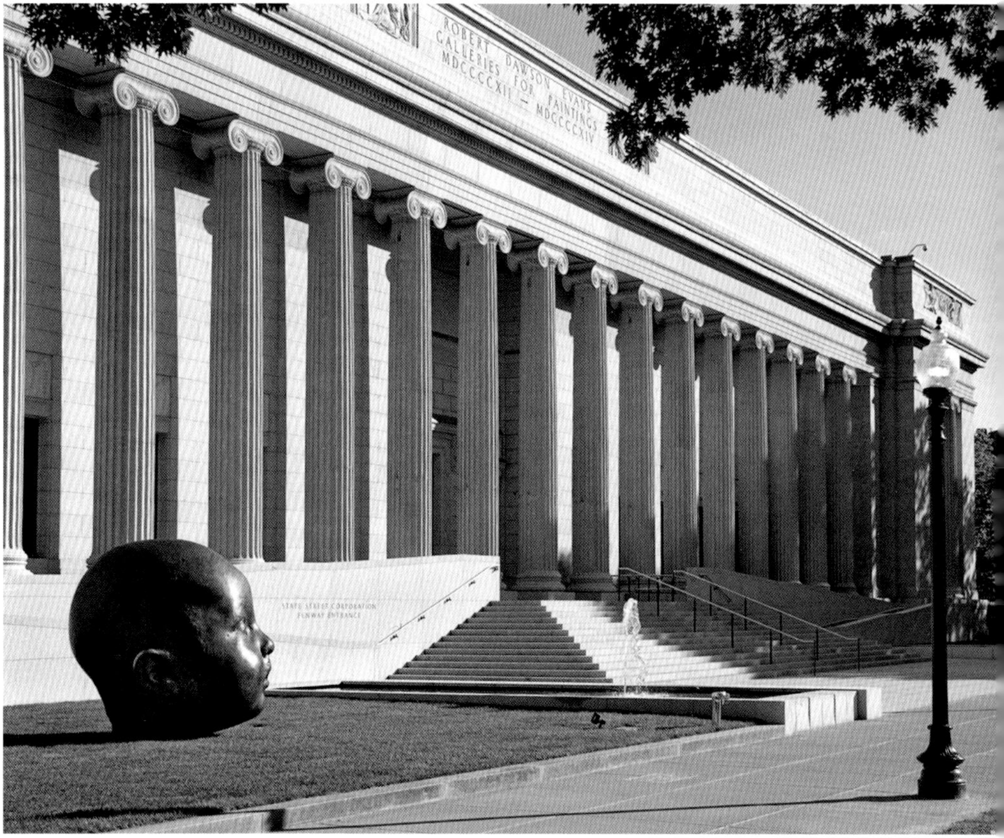

Overleaf: The North Pavilion of the Art of the Americas Wing seen from the Back Bay Fens. The landscape overlooking the Fens has been renovated and the entrance approach redesigned to encourage visitors to enter the museum from the north.

Facts and figures

Museum of Fine Arts, Boston
Boston, USA
1999–2010

Client
Museum of Fine Arts, Boston

Project Team
Norman Foster
Spencer de Grey
Michael Jones
Kate Murphy
John Small
William Castagna

Bénédicte Artault
Robin Blanchard
Jan Coghlan
Chris Connell
Aaron Davis
Gennaro di Dato
James Edwards
Dagmar Eisenach
Morgan Fleming
Kristin Fox
Herbert Gsottbauer
Anthony Guma
Sean Hanna
Rie Haslov
Judith Kernt
Ismael Juan Khan
Kohelika Kohli
Phyllis Lam
Abel Maciel
Peter Matcham
Pablo Menendez Paz
Aidan Monaghan
Yat Lun Ng
Mathis Osterhage
Silvia Paredes
Carol Patterson
Michael Pelken
Michael Richter
Katherine Ridley
Il Hoon Roh
Ingrid Sölken
Matthew Stokes
Diego Suarez
Jane Tiley
Hans-Christian Wilhelm
Alexis Williams
Oliver Wong
Richard Yates

Consultants
Architect of Record: CBT/Childs Bertman Tseckares Inc
Design Structural Engineers: Buro Happold
Structural Engineers of Record: Weidlinger Associates
Cost Consultant: Davis Langdon
Design MEP Engineers: Buro Happold
MEP Engineers of Record: WSP Flack + Kurtz
Landscape Architect: Gustafson Guthrie Nichol
General Contractor: John Moriarty & Associates
Pre-Construction Services: George BH Macomber Company
Enabling Contractor: Skanska USA Building Inc
Environmental Consultant: Epsilon Associates
Geotechnical Consultant: McPhail Associates Inc
Civil Engineers: Nitsch Engineering Inc
Permitting: Goulston & Storrs
Code Consultant: Hughes Associates
Transport Consultant: Howard/Stein-Hudson Associates
Lighting Consultant: George Sexton Associates
Acoustic & AV Consultant: Acentech Inc
Signage and Wayfinding: Roll Barresi & Associates Inc
External Envelope Consultant: Simpson Gumpertz & Heger Inc
Security Consultant: Ducibella Venter & Santore
Hardware Consultant: IR Security & Safety Consultants of New England
Space Planning: Robert Luchetti Associates Inc
Pedestrian Flow Consultant: Orca Consulting Group
Elevator Consultant: Van Deusen & Associates

Principal Awards
2011 Preservation Achievement Award, Boston Preservation Alliance
2011 RIBA International Award
2012 Boston Society of Architects' People's Choice Award

Project timeline

1876 4 July: Museum of Fine Arts, Boston, opens at Copley Square in a building designed by architects John Hubbard Sturgis and Charles Brigham; the building is home to 5,600 works of art

1909 May: the Copley Square building closes
November: the MFA opens a new Beaux-Arts building on Huntington Avenue, designed by Boston architect Guy Lowell

1915 February: the Evans Wing for Paintings opens, completing the second phase of Guy Lowell's original masterplan

1925 Artist John Singer Sargent completes an ambitious mural programme, which incorporates sculpture and architectural ornamentation for the MFA's Rotunda (completed 1925) and Colonnade, now known as the Ruth and Carl J Shapiro Rotunda and Colonnade; these murals are restored and conserved in 1999

1927 September: the School of the Museum of Fine Arts opens its new building, designed by Guy Lowell, on the Fenway

1928 November: the Decorative Arts Wing, designed by Guy Lowell, opens on the east side of the MFA to house the museum's extensive collection of European and American decorative arts

1970 June: the George Robert White Wing, designed by Hugh Stubbins, opens on the western side of the MFA, providing new space for a conservation laboratory, a library, restaurants, education facilities and administrative offices

1981 July: the West Wing, designed by IM Pei, opens; it incorporates a large gallery space for special exhibitions, an auditorium, restaurants and shops

1999 March: Foster + Partners is commissioned to develop the masterplan for the development of the MFA

2001 September: the museum launches the 'Building the New MFA' campaign

2002 February: the masterplan proposals are presented

2005 November: the new building project breaks ground

2006 September: the MFA names the Art of the Ancient World Wing in honour of George D and Margo Behrakis

2008 June: the MFA opens the State Street Corporation Fenway Entrance, which had been closed since the early 1980s, as well as a new Jean S and Frederic A Sharf Visitor Center; the IM Pei-designed West Wing is renamed the Linde Family Wing for Contemporary Art
September: the MFA concludes Building the New MFA campaign, raising $504 million; the placement of the final steel beam in the new building is marked with a topping out ceremony

2009 April: the renovation of the Huntington Avenue Entrance on the Avenue of the Arts is completed
November: the new building work is completed

2010 20 November: the Art of the Americas Wing and Ruth and Carl J Shapiro Family Courtyard open to the public with a free Community Day, which attracts 13,500 visitors
The museum is now home to 450,000 works of art

2011 September: the Linde Family Wing for Contemporary Art opens in the former West Wing

Vital statistics

Visitor numbers
- 2011 – 1,202,531
- 2010 – 876,605
- 2009 – 961,148

Funding
- The $345 million project was supported by a fundraising campaign that raised $504 million for new construction and renovations, endowment of programmes and positions, and annual operations

Pre-construction area
- 483,447 square feet/44,914 square metres

Demolished building area
- 59,835 square feet/5,559 square metres

New construction area
- 193,325 square feet/17,960 square metres

MFA total building area
- 616,937 square feet/57,315 square metres – a 28 per cent increase

MFA total gallery area
- 221,267 square feet/20,556 square metres

Art of the Americas Wing

Building height
- 70 feet/21 metres

Number of storeys
- Three gallery levels above ground; one gallery level below ground

Total gallery area
- 51,338 square feet/4,770 square metres – a 42 per cent increase over previous gallery space for the Art of the Americas collections

Number of galleries
- 53 rooms, ranging from 700 to 1,800 square feet/65 to 167 square metres; plus the installation of an additional nine period rooms

Height of galleries
- 15 feet/4.57 metres typically
- 22 feet/6.7 metres on the upper floor

Number of works on display
- Approximately 5,000 works – more than double the number of American objects previously displayed

Shapiro Family Courtyard
- The Courtyard is enclosed by a new freestanding building; a multi-purpose 'living room' it provides a space for art displays and events, with a new café and seating
- 121,840 square feet/11,319 square metres
- 63 feet /4.87 metres high

Ann and Graham Gund Gallery
- A flexible 'black box' beneath the Courtyard, for major special exhibitions, including a new shop at the exit
- 8,280 square feet/769 square metres

Education Center
- The 150-seat, multi-purpose Barbara and Theodore Alfond Auditorium for film, speech and music; two studio classrooms and one seminar room
- 4,300 square feet/400 square metres

Sharf Visitor Center
- 4,920 square feet/457 square metres

Environmental initiatives

The use of daylight, as far as it is permitted by the display of works of art, reduces artificial lighting demands

The energy-efficient lighting system is connected to light and motion sensors, and efficient centralised HVAC systems

Triple glazing minimises thermal transmission and sun-shading devices reduce the need for mechanical cooling

Sanitary fittings with low flow-rates, including PIR sensing taps, reduce water consumption by 25 per cent

The landscaping is designed to minimise irrigation, using species that require minimal or no watering

The storm-water management system is designed to capture rainwater and allow slow infiltration into the sewer network, thus reducing the risk of flooding

The MFA is committed to reducing car usage by taking advantage of the MBTA tram stop in front of the building; the MFA also offers a 25 per cent subsidy on monthly MBTA passes to its staff, provides bicycle parking in the garage and charges market-rate parking fees

Guy Lowell and the MFA

A native Bostonian, Guy Lowell (1870-1927) graduated from Harvard College in 1892, and gained a degree in architecture from MIT in 1894. He subsequently studied landscape and horticulture at the Royal Botanic Gardens, Kew, and architectural history and landscape architecture under Jean-Louis Pascal at the École des Beaux-Arts in Paris.

Lowell established his own highly successful practice in Boston on his return to the United States in 1899. By 1906 he had opened a second office in New York and divided his time between the two cities. His work included large public, academic and commercial buildings alongside numerous houses, country estates and formal gardens.

In 1907 the trustees of the MFA commissioned Lowell to devise a masterplan for a building that could be completed in stages as funding became available. The first section of Lowell's Neoclassical design, including the Rotunda, was completed in 1909 and featured a facade of cut granite than ran for 500 feet (152 metres) along Huntington Avenue.

The second phase, the wing along the Back Bay Fens, opened in 1915 and originally housed painting galleries. From 1916 to 1925 the artist John Singer Sargent was commissioned to create the murals and other works of art that line the Rotunda and the Colonnade.

In addition to the MFA, Lowell is chiefly remembered for the design of the New York County Courthouse, completed in 1927. Other notable works include the Lowell Lecture Hall at Harvard, and buildings at Phillips Academy, Andover, Simmons College, and Brown University. He also worked on the Charles River esplanades in collaboration with the landscape architect Charles Eliot.

Lowell was also an influential teacher, founding and running the highly respected landscape architecture programme at MIT from 1900 to 1910.

The Secrets
Outlook:
THE
BOSTON
The Calderwood

Credits

Editor: David Jenkins
Design: Thomas Manss & Company; Thomas Manss, Angela Pescolderung
Picture Research: Gayle Mault, Lauren Catten
Proofreading: Julia Dawson, Rebecca Roke
Production Supervision: Martin Lee
Reproduction: Dawkins Colour
Printed and bound in Italy by Grafiche SiZ S.p.A.

The FSC®-certified paper GardaMatt has been supplied by Cartiere del Garda S.p.A., Italy

Picture credits

Photographs
Richard Bryant/Arcaid: 88-89
Chuck Choi: 36, 44, 62-63, 68, 69, 74-75, 76, 77, 84, 85, 94-95
Foster + Partners: 16, 20, 21,
MFA, Boston: 14, 17, 18, 59, 60, 61, 87
David L Ryan/Boston Globe: 40, 41, 82
Nigel Young/Foster + Partners: 6-7, 22-23, 24, 25, 26, 27, 30, 31, 32-33, 35, 37, 38, 39, 45, 46, 47, 48, 49, 52, 53, 54-55, 56, 57, 58, 64, 65, 66-67, 70-71, 72, 73, 78-79, 86

Drawings
Birds Portchmouth Russum: 28-29, 42-43
Norman Foster: 4-5,
Foster + Partners: 19, 50, 51, 80, 81
Gregory Gibbon: 12-13, 34, 83

Joel Shapiro, *Untitled* 1997, courtesy of ARS NY and DACS London, 2013; Zhan Wang *Artificial Rock #85*, courtesy of Long March Space and the artist; Antonio López García, *Day* and *Night*, courtesy of the artist.

Every effort has been made to contact copyright holders. The publishers apologise for any omissions, which they will be pleased to rectify at the earliest opportunity.

Editor's Note

In editing this book I am particularly grateful to Norman Foster and Edward R Bosley for their invaluable contributions. I would also like to thank Malcolm Rogers and his staff at the MFA; Thomas Manss and Angela Pescolderung for graphic design; Rebecca Roke for editorial and research support; Gayle Mault and Lauren Catten for picture research; Julia Dawson for proofreading; Martin Lee and John Bodkin for coordinating production; and the many people in the Foster studio – particularly Spencer de Grey and Michael Jones – who helped to piece together the background to the project.

David Jenkins
London, January 2013